THE FIRST YES

REDISCOVERING THE INTEGRITY OF THE CALL TO PREACH

BY

KENNETH Q. JAMES

The First Yes
by Kenneth Q. James

Printed in the United States of America

ISBN 9781609572853

www.xulonpress.com

ACKNOWLEDGEMENTS

Writing this book and seeing it come to reality is a dream come true. It reflects the deepest beliefs that I hold as a preacher, teacher, pastor and Christian. They have, as are most deeply held convictions, been developed over time. Many of them have not come to me easily; they were won through hard fought encounters, conflicts with those of different opinions or visions and ultimately, the scaffolding of support that has undergirded my entire life.

So it is incumbent upon me to express words of thanks to the people who have across the years and throughout my journey made the contributions that have brought this book to fruition.

I have enjoyed the support of my family throughout my life. Many of the dearest people to me on my journey are now of sainted memory. They may be gone, but they are certainly not forgotten, for I carry them in my heart each day, and not one day goes by that one or all of them don't come to mind for some purpose of reflection, or just so that I can feel and sense the support that I am sure they would certainly give and the words of advice I am confident they would offer.

With fond memories, I dedicate this book to family members now deceased: my mother, Joan E. James, my grandmother, Brunhilda M. Simmons, my great-grandmother and great-grandfather, Daisy Kenney and Paul Kenney.

I am grateful to the many Christian educators, Sunday school teachers and advisors throughout my life who gave of their time, talent and effort to nurture me in the faith that I now hold so dear.

I am indebted to Reverend George W. McMurray who presided as pastor over my life and the lives of my family during the years of my youth as a member of Mother A.M.E. Zion Church. During that time, my faith was cultivated by the continuing and hands on guidance of several who served as ministers to the youth: Reverends Peter A. Price, Sherman Lewis, Choyce Hall, and S. Chuka Ekemam (now Bishop), to name a few.

I recall fondly and with deep gratitude the godly wisdom and judgment of Bishop Herbert Bell Shaw who ordained me into the ministry; Bishop Ruben L. Speaks, who assigned me to my first pastoral charge and ordained me as an elder; Bishop J. Clinton Hoggard, Bishop George W.C. Walker and Bishop George E. Battle, Jr., who in the subsequent appointments I received and through the responsibilities with which I was increasingly entrusted, helped me to grow and develop into maturity as a preacher and pastor.

I have been blessed with significant and valued friendships, too many to name here each one individually, but some will stand out for their fidelity, endurance and encouragement through the years: Dr. Reginald D. Broadnax, Reverend Dr. W. Darin Moore, Pastor Darius G. Pridgen Reverend Douglas L. Maven and Reverend Dr. Raymon Hunt. A special thanks to Reverend Dr. Alvin T. Durant, Sr., who took the time to read my work and advise me as I was completing my work at Hood Seminary for the Doctor of Ministry degree. I am also indebted to countless colleagues for conversations about preaching and critique of my thoughts which serve to strengthen and make me better and which foster (sometimes by force) my continuing maturity.

Those who know me now may not know the names or contributions of some of these persons, but they must know as I do that I do not come to this point made, but because of the input and involvement of such invaluable persons, I am being made.

Finally, I offer thanks to the person whom I consider the most important person in my life, my son, Frank. Because of you, I have a fuller understanding of what love, caring, understanding and patience can do to transform an individual.

Contents

Chapter 1

The Integrity of Preaching

"'What can I say that will reach these worriers?" broods the poor clergyman. He knows about many anxieties in the pews, but how about his own? He, too, is worried and troubled. His salary is small, his youngest daughter is unhappy, the clerk of the session is disagreeable, the 'ministry of music' is presumptuous, and there are dissident factions in the education department. Each Sunday morning there are more empty seats. Is he at fault or is it the times? Nevertheless, he must go on and preach and really say something. What shall he say to these people? Scold them? Warn them? Tell them that he is worried, too? Bless them and urge them to pray? Promise them peace? Should he, like Moses, cover his face so as not to look too holy? God is good, he

> could remind them; God means well for all of us; He has promised us His grace; He has forgiven us already. It is darkest just before dawn. So the Lord bless you and keep you...make His face to shine... and please, will you all come back again next week?"[1]

I love preaching. I love everything about it, beginning with reading the text, the research and study of the text, constructing the sermon, discussing the ideas that I glean from reading the text with my colleagues, reading and reviewing what I have written and then finally, actually preaching the sermon. I believe the privilege of preaching the gospel of Jesus Christ is the greatest joy that anyone can have. Preaching is my passion in life.

[1] Karl Menninger, M.D., *Whatever Became of Sin?* Hawthorn Books, NY, 1973. P. 195

The best way I can describe this passion for preaching is to use the model of the prophet Jeremiah (Jeremiah 1:5): "Before I formed you in the womb I knew you, before you were born I set you apart; I appointed you as a prophet to the nations." This is simply to say that the prophet Jeremiah was born to prophesy, or to preach. The skill set he had could have been used in many other disciplines or careers, and he may well have even been effective at them. However, I doubt that he would have been happy in those pursuits because preaching, prophesying, is what Jeremiah was born to do. This is the way I feel about myself and my call, and why I agree with William Barclay when he says, "There are two great beginnings in the life of every man who has left his mark upon history. There is the day when he is born into the world; and there is the day when he discovers why he was born into the world."[2]

As preachers and as pastors, we acquire, develop and nurture skills that would serve us well in many areas. Sometimes we have the opportunity to use those experiences in the larger society. I have heard some preachers say that if they took a job in the secular world they would discover that they are grossly underpaid in the work of ministry, given the responsibility, experience and requirements of the job we are often asked to perform. That may be true, but can anything else we do ever come close to the satisfaction we find in preaching God's word?

[2] William Barclay, *The Mind of Jesus*, Harper Collins Publishers, 1960. P.3

For me, the answer is no. This is a value that preachers must convey and share both with the generation of preachers following us now, as well as to our congregations and the people we serve, so that all may appreciate what it means to preach the gospel. We come to do what we do, not for the rewards and benefits, but because we feel compelled to do so. This is the essence of what we talk about when we say we are "called."

Because I love preaching, I take it seriously. I am frankly impatient with those who do not. Some in the pew as well as (sadly) in the pulpit approach the gospel too casually for my taste. To some in the pulpit, preaching is nothing more than a way to earn a living, or some means of showing off one's oratorical talents. To some in the pew, preaching is at best an unnecessary verbal exercise about what they believe they already know, and at worst, a colossal waste of time. It is sad that there are those who have such a dim view of this glorious responsibility. I attribute this mindset to the lack of purpose or loss of focus on what the gospel and preaching are really all about.

I do not mean to present myself as some kind of expert on preaching. I doubt, really, that there is any such thing. In fact, the best preachers I know and have heard would be the last to offer themselves as experts on the subject or even dare to suggest that they are particularly savvy about the craft of preaching. It is here that the greatest difficulty of preaching emerges. In any other successful endeavor in life, credit is taken and readily available, viewed as a direct result of hard, work, craftsmanship and diligence. The best in their field will claim and demand the rewards of their industry, and rightfully so. Preachers have no such right. When our best sermons are preached, when we have made a "name" for ourselves as fine expositors of the gospel, when our churches grow and people flock from all around to hear us "tell the story," the only right and proper thing for us to do is to remind ourselves and our listeners that "we have this treasure in jars of clay to show that this all-surpassing power is from God and not from us" (2 Corinthians 4:7).

It's not hard to lose that perspective, you know. When people greet you at the door of the sanctuary and tell you every week how good and wonderful and gifted you are or how clearly you spoke to their need, it takes a Herculean effort of humility not to get caught up in that praise, or as my mother used to say, "to not believe your own press clippings." So when the congregation does not meet our expectations, or the appointment does not fit our perception of self-image, and if (gasp!) the honorarium is not appropriate to my set of gifts and graces and station and place in ministry, is it any wonder that we get offended and tell ourselves that from now on those who invite us must meet a certain criteria so that we are treated "fairly" and right? I do not mean this solely as a criticism of those who can command a certain figure before their invitation to preach is secured, because I do believe that "the worker deserves his wages" (1 Timothy 5:18). There is a question I want to raise for consideration, preacher: is the big honorarium, the prestigious appointment or the high profile speaking engagement the reason you went into the ministry? Did you get caught up in the apparent glamour of the profile of a personality and now your intentions have been diverted? The late Bishop Ruben Speaks used to tell us that one way to know if you love what you do is to ask if you would do it for free; do you love the gospel that much that you would preach it without pay – or as Jesus put it (Matthew 10:8), "Freely you have received, freely give?" Or is the worth and value of your ministry all about clothing, cars, money and the trappings of success? Now, don't get nervous, preacher, I am not suggesting that you clean out your closet and give away all your suits, or that you sell your car and drive a hybrid. But I do think it is worth considering why we do what we do. The answers to questions such as these will bring us to the heart or the integrity of preaching, and no one has the answer to those questions but you as you search the deepest motives of your heart.

There is both an art and a diligence that is required to keep preaching fresh. The diligence required for preaching will allow the ministers in the pews to recapture an appreciation for preaching. Most people probably don't know nor have any idea what is required for a sermon to be preached effectively, the time involved in the preparation and the necessary elements that all must come together for the delivery of the message to be effective. But for the person who listens to a sermon, isn't it is sort of like going to a fine five star restaurant and enjoying a meal prepared by a top chef? While I may not know every ingredient or understand the combination that makes the recipe or all of the effort that goes into preparing the meal, I can be satisfied with a good meal when it is served.

I don't have any fears that preaching will ultimately die as a means of communication, nor that people, in general, will ultimately tire of hearing the gospel message. Our abilities, even considering all our frailties and shortcomings are still not weak enough to negate the purpose and power of the gospel. Even if we do a poor job of representing – or *re*-presenting – the God of the Bible, there is no worry here that God is limited by our deficiencies. Quite the contrary, it is the miracle of all miracles that the gospel is effective in spite of our failings and shortcomings. Every time we stand to preach, God miraculously overcomes our lack of interest, failure to prepare properly, slowness of speech and personal issues and agendas and someone leaves having heard "a word from the Lord." In that marvelous moment when God has spoken, no glory for that belongs to any man or woman; it is nothing short of God's amazing intervention of grace that brings it to pass.

I believe that there is an integrity to preaching that must never diminish. The integrity of preaching cannot be secondary or tertiary in one's approach, falling somewhere on the agenda after our desire for fame and notoriety and what often passes for success in our culture. Preaching cannot be reduced to an exercise where one stands to prove how eloquent he is, or how learned she is above the dullards who occupy the pews. If that is the motive of preaching, it is no wonder preaching has lost its luster in our churches. People with healthy self-esteem would soon grow bored of listening to such showmanship. No matter what the gifts and abilities, no well adjusted individual can stand (or should be willing) to listen to another person talk about themselves perpetually, conceitedly, brashly, week after week as if the speaker has or is the answer to the difficulties another faces in his or her life. If as preachers we present ourselves as the kind of people who live "six feet above contradiction" it is no wonder the listeners soon grow disinterested. I seek and call for an integrity in preaching that speaks of an honesty born of humility as I recognize my frailty in offering myself as God's instrument, and a thankfulness and gratitude that rises from the knowledge that I – least of all persons, knowing what a mess I am – should ever have this privilege of preaching God's word. As the Apostle Paul said, "Although I am the very least of all the saints, this grace was given to me to bring to the Gentiles the news of the boundless riches of Christ" (Ephesians 3:8, NRSV).

It is not impossible to recover this integrity. It means that we must return to the roots of our calling. How, why and for what reason did we begin the journey as preachers? The answer is not complicated: we heard the Word of God.

Upon hearing God's word, we were convinced of its eternal value and purpose. We were sure that this Word would give us something, that a word from God would say something to us that would be life changing, life affirming and life giving. At some point then, we heard "the call" – a call which the A.M.E. Zion Book of Discipline describes as "internal and external."

1. The internal call consists of those gifts and graces requisite to the proper and faithful discharge of the duties of the Christian ministry. We expect those who profess to be moved upon by the Holy Ghost to preach; (1) To evince an unmistakable conception of salvation by faith; (2) To possess a sound mind; (3) To have a clear understanding of the Scriptures; (4) To have a right judgment in the things of God; (5) To have a good degree of utterance as a Preacher.
2. The external call does not confer personal gifts nor qualifications, but presupposes both. It is designed to confer upon the Preacher who is

> found to possess the inward call, official authority, to exercise in the name of God and in the name of the Church, the functions of Christian Ministry.[3]

The integrity of preaching for many preachers has been lost in the desire to impress the listeners, or our colleagues, or make a name for ourselves or imitate some icon in the media galaxy of preaching success. These are the kind of misguided pursuits and feckless desires that makes preaching ultimately uninteresting to the audience it attempts to reach. The preaching of the gospel is never about the person delivering the message; it is always, first and foremost about the God who is at the center of the story. We heard the call of God in our lives, answered

[3] *2000 A.M.E. Zion Book of Discipline*, Qualifications and Rules for a Preacher. P.73, par. 188

that call and responded with no desire to be anything other than God's vessel. We can and must recover this integrity for this and future generations. If we lose it altogether, it would mean that preachers would enter the ministry for reasons nothing less than mercenary. We may already be on a fast track to that awful result now, as preachers and congregations measure, compare and compete for who has the biggest, best and/or the most of some arbitrary measurement. And in the midst of these impractical pursuits, the integrity of preaching has been lost.

The integrity of preaching will restore our ministries to the reason we gave initially for answering the call of God. That response to that integrity was discovered in one simple word – "yes." Sadly, the reason we first said "yes" when we heard God's call has taken a back seat to our own selfish agendas. There was a purity and unsullied principle in the quest of our response that we must recapture. There was, we presume, a purity of our motives that led us to make sacrifices and commitments to ministry, and in a spirit of surrender we gave to God this initial, unqualified "yes." When we lose that integrity, preaching is not only often erroneous in its purpose; it is nearly always lacking joy and is just plain no longer fun, for both the pulpit and the pew. It is a chore to be done by the preacher or suffered through by the parishioner.

There are too many hurts and pains that one will suffer in the course of doing the will of God to engage in ministry for any other reason than because ultimately God will be glorified.

We are guaranteed disappointments in life and ministry, and to think that we can avoid them is foolish and deceptive. It always surprises me when members and ministers walk away from the church because they have been wounded or hurt by circumstances or by people. It makes you wonder what they expected. We have lost, it seems, the sentiment in the church and ministry conveyed by the great hymn writer, Isaac Watts, who wrote,

Must I be carried to the skies On flowery beds of ease,
While others fought to win the prize, And sailed through bloody seas?

Are there no foes for me to face? Must I not stem the flood?
Is this vile world a friend to grace, To help me on to God?

Sure I must fight if I would reign; Increase my courage, Lord.
I'll bear the toil, endure the pain, Supported by Thy Word.

Never at any point have we been given the idea that our lives should be trouble free, not in our daily walk and certainly not in ministry. People are going to be insensitive and sometimes downright mean. We will have visions that they will refuse to help bring to fruition. At those moments, we don't have the choice of picking up our toys and going home; we are going to have to remind ourselves of what we promised God we would do. Such times will call for a greater resolve than acting on emotion, with a "tit for tat" response that leaves the church and people we serve poorer. At the heart of the integrity of ministry is found the preacher who must be a person of character, integrity and moral fiber. The preacher must be a person whose words move people into action, either by challenge or inspiration. The preacher has a unique and grave responsibility upon his or her shoulders. Preaching and preachers are important to the very fabric of our society and the makeup of the church, as it is God's means of moving men and women into the understanding of God's will and the kingdom of God.

This is also why telling God "yes" is dangerous. Don't say yes to God if you don't mean it. You will be challenged, criticized, condemned, castigated, chewed out, chastened and censured. But as I remember the reason I promised God I would go, when I get back to the heart of the integrity of ministry, I can say as the Apostle Paul said (Acts 20:24, KJV): "But none of these things move me, neither count I my life dear unto myself, so that I might finish my course with joy, and the ministry, which I have received of the Lord Jesus, to testify the gospel of the grace of God."

I once thought that we should undertake the task of saving the church. I have attended and shared in all kinds of groups, committees, conferences and seminars where we coalesce and discuss "what is wrong with the church." Of course, we have some sure-fire solutions for how to fix what we believe is wrong. We criticize, sometimes benignly and sometimes with venomous intent, the leadership and direction of those in seats of authority – bishops, elders, pastors, lay leaders. That seems to me now to be a fruitless and unproductive enterprise. I do not believe that it is possible nor are we capable to make the wholesale changes that we dream and discuss. Rather, we need to focus on the one element that we can change - ourselves. The task of fixing what is wrong with the church may be too tall an order for any of us as individuals to take on. I think that our real goal should be how we can save our individual ministries, and as a result, we may be able to save the church. We should be able to handle that much. This is why integrity of preaching is so important.

CHAPTER 2

UNDERSTANDING "THE FIRST YES"

When a man realizes that he has been
entrusted with a grave responsibility,
he cannot act as if it did not matter how he
discharged it. Always he feels the spur of
another's trust and confidence. To remember
that another depends on him, has placed
his confidence in him, helps to keep a man
responsible and true to his trust.[4]

Each and every time I stand to preach, I want to remember or reignite the fire that

[4] David A. MacLennon, *Entrusted With the Gospel,* The Westminster Press, 1951. P. 31-32

first brought me to the floor at the Class Meeting at Mother A.M.E. Zion Church on July 16, 1975. On reflection, I realize that I was totally unprepared for what I was about to do, for where this "yes" that I said to God was going to take me. The prospect of what it meant to be a preacher was on that day, at least, ill-considered. I had not the faintest idea what such a thing really meant or what I was about to do with it. I may not have realized it at the time, but this has turned out to be a journey, not the quick, snap decision that I or others may have thought it to be, and now some thirty years later, I am still trying to figure this all out. But there was one thing about which I was completely convinced - God had spoken to me and told me to preach His word, and I was committed to do so. Even if I said "yes" before I fully understood what that "yes" meant, the fact is, I said "yes." And that "yes" is one on which I have no desire to renege. I made a vow to the Lord and I won't take it back. With all the confusion, questions and issues that I have had to wrestle with since, I never want to renege on that yes, even as I am still trying to understand it.

A few years ago I had the most unfortunate experience to have a kidney stone. On the day that I passed the kidney stone and took it to the urologist who wanted to examine it, I remember wondering to myself how something so small could cause so much discomfort. For several weeks, although I did my best to mask the pain, it was clear to everyone who saw me that I was not feeling well. No matter how I tried not to show it, the discomfort was apparent in my expressions and my movement. I kept my preaching engagements and fulfilled my pastoral obligations, and there was no let up in my schedule. But I was hurting. After a few days or weeks of bravely trudging through, I knew I needed to seek help from an informed source, a doctor.

As I reflect on this now and the lessons that kidney stone taught me, I wonder: Could it be that God allows, even creates, the tension and discomfort we sometimes feel, so that we will seek the help we need to get back on track? For me, the pain and misery of having this kidney stone, though it was in fact small, eventually forced me to put my schedule and plans on hold and seek help. It may be that preachers and churches are at a crossroads where we must deal with the pain and discomfort experienced and expressed by persons in the church's ministry who are uncomfortable with the status quo and are seeking help. To do this will take the kind of courage about which Paul Tillich wrote, a courage that is "the ultimate source of the courage to be (which) is the 'God above God.'"[5]

Obviously there is risk involved here. Who wants to be the unpopular voice that screams that the emperor has no clothes? When everyone else in the crowd either sees nothing wrong with the situation or is too fearful to speak because of the implied or real reprisals, where do you find the strength and the courage to be the voice, as it

[5] Paul Tillich, "The Courage to Be," Yale University Press, 1952. P. 186

were, of one "crying in the wilderness?" Tillich continues,

> There should be no question of what Christian theology has to do in this situation. It should decide for truth against safety, even if safety is consecrated and supported by the churches.[6]

An arrogance that believes that you have already reached the zenith of your ability and the understanding of God's ways leads to a dead end. There is so much about God I do not know as God reveals more of God to me every day, so I must be open, available, and prepared to hear what God is saying and where God is leading. What I know about God has been wonderful and sufficient for the journey to this

[6] Ibid., p.141

point. What I need to know about God is ready to be manifested to my understanding if I don't close the avenues to that revelation thinking I already know enough. I know there is risk involved in finding that deeper place where God calls, but it is a risk worth taking if you are going to know God.

The story of Jacob wrestling with the angel in Genesis 32 comes to mind. It always seemed strange to me that an angel wrestles with Jacob all night, and only as the day breaks does the angel try to get away. Who was this angel that Jacob wrestled? Some say it was not an angel but in fact, God Himself. The text seems to bear out this premise, as Jacob later calls the place Peniel, for he said (Genesis 32:30) "It is because I saw God face to face, and yet my life was spared."

If in fact Jacob was wrestling with God, then it makes sense that God would graciously seek to end the wrestling match. In the darkness, Jacob had no idea what he was dealing with. But as the day broke, Jacob would discover who his wrestling partner is, and since as God later revealed to Moses (Exodus 33:20) "You cannot see my face, for no one may see me and live," it seems that by saying "Let me go it is daybreak" God was trying to save Jacob's life. If Jacob continued to this wrestling match until the daylight revealed with whom he was wrestling, he would not have lived to tell the story. But Jacob was so desperate for the next level – "the God above God?" as Tillich describes it – that apparently he thought it was worth the risk, and so he would not let go. He was rewarded with an encounter that changed his life.

Even if one argues that preaching ministry is generally in good shape and healthy (an argument you are most likely to hear by those positioned to benefit from the church's rewards, which I will discuss later), it must be acknowledged that "Just as a generally healthy person tends to ignore going to the doctor, a healthy church tends not to gather the hard truth by asking, 'How are we *really* doing?[7]

Understanding what our "yes" means will take us places we might have avoided for some time in our pursuits of things other than God's

[7] H. Dale Burke, *Even Healthy Churches Need to Change,* Leadership, Fall, 2005, Vol. XXVI, Number 4, Marshall Shelley, editor

perfect will for our lives and ministries. It may require some painful and difficult confessions, even repentance. But if there is to be fulfillment, joy and integrity in our ministry, this step is unavoidable.

If we look at Genesis chapters 1-3, it is intriguing to follow the discussion that takes place between God, Adam and Eve. Follow what God said to the man and to the woman, as well as what the man and woman said to each other. What caught my attention is in the first two chapters, there is no record of anything that the man or the woman said *to* God. God gave instructions, and those instructions were apparently followed clearly, precisely, specifically and without error. The first conversation or words spoken by the man and the woman to

God directly occur only when another voice is introduced into the narrative. When in Genesis 3 the serpent reinterprets what God has said and causes the man and the woman to disobey, we find the first words recorded that are spoken by man and woman directly to God. And those first words spoken are very telling and spoke clearly to me: "I heard you in the garden and I was afraid because I was naked; so I hid" (Genesis 3:10).

"I heard you," Adam said.

These words from Adam indicate that the instructions God gave were clear. There were no questions about them or misunderstanding of the directive, and so apparently there was no need for conversation, clarification or confirmation. Adam knew what was to be done, and with that understanding he said, "Yes." When caught in disobedience, he made clear that he understood the instructions: "I heard you," Adam said. He essentially confesses to God, "I know what it is you told me to do. I was afraid and I hid because when I followed another voice it caused me to disobey your orders. I hid because I couldn't face you knowing that I had disobeyed."

I know how Adam felt. I have let others define ministry for me for too long. I had been told how to preach, how to look, with whom to keep company, how to get ahead only to finally discover that all of those instructions are not getting me anywhere. It was pulling me away from the voice that called me and to which I first said "yes." I had to take seriously the task of correcting the misdirection of my ministry. Now, hearing the voice of God as I tried to hide, God is graciously inviting me now to do what God invited Moses to do in Exodus 3:5 – "take off your sandals, for the place where you are standing is holy ground." Marc Gafni makes an observation on this passage that helped me find clarity.

> The foot print, like the fingerprint and palm print, is a physical expression of the soul print. Reflexologists and foot doctors will tell you that no foot is the same...Have you ever pondered the difference between the print you leave when you're wearing a shoe and the print you leave with a bare foot? The print left by your Nike is the same print left by every Nike, but the print left by your foot is unique to you.[8]

[8] Marc Gafni *Soul Prints,* Pocket Books, New York, 2001. P. 219-220

This serves as a call for me to be quite specific and clear about what shape my ministry will take. I must find the distinguishing characteristic of my ministry. No more copycat imitations, no more counterfeit pretenses, no more "going along to get along" all the while going nowhere. In heeding the call like the one God invited Moses to share by taking off his shoes, and responding to that call by saying "yes," God's invitation intends that the place where Moses or I or anyone meets and encounters God would leave a mark that is definitive and that we will recognize. When I take off my shoes on the ground where I do ministry, I will leave a mark that cannot be erased.

A troubling aspect of this commitment is to discover that I will probably not receive much help or guidance from others in seeking to define myself and my ministry. I have received a lot of suggestions about how to live out my call and become what some would define as a "good minister."

> A *good* minister? What is that? A massive study conducted by the Association of Theological Schools discovered that, apart from an almost universal agreement on integrity of character and ability to get along well with people, there is no broad consensus in the American church on what a good minister is or ought to be.[9]

The suggestions have often been helpful sometimes, but other times they have been, well frankly, quite ridiculous and absurd. They have been suggestions that have tried to fit me into a mold, and someone else's mold

[9] Ronald E. Osborn, *Creative Disarray: Models of Ministry in a Changing America,* Chalice Press, 1991. P. 3

at that, which is if not impossible, at the very least uncomfortable. David figured that out when Saul tried to get him to wear his armor (1 Samuel 17). When David goes to fight this giant Goliath, Saul decides how David should go fight this battle. But what Saul suggests is a grievous error; he tries to suit David up in armor that Saul would wear. David, of course, rejects it, and I always thought it was because David was unaccustomed to wearing the military regalia that Saul would have liked to see him wear, but there is perhaps another, deeper meaning. Saul is attempting to have David fight with the same weapons that the enemy is using – Goliath has armor, a helmet, a coat of mail and a sword, so that is what Saul wants David to use. David realizes, even his the tender age and while still a young man, that there is no use in fighting God's battles if I'm going to use the same tools as the enemy. So he puts them off, removes them, says he is not used to them, and rejects any reliance on this kind of power as false and deceptive. David fights the fight on his terms and uses tools with which he is comfortable, and God takes up the battle with him and gives him the victory. David had to be himself, and realizes quite significantly that he could not expect to get God's victory if he was going to use the same tools as the enemy Goliath, or the tools that others expected him to use.

This raises a question that every one of us must answer. Who – or what – shaped you, dressed you or prepared you to become who and what we are in ministry today? It seems we have more in common with Adam in the Garden of Eden than we realize. Whose is that interfering voice that I am hearing that has now caused me to "hide" in my ministry? Tradition? Fear? Authority? Personal gain? Advancement? What has made me disobey that first "yes" that I heard?

Let me say one thing, and about this I want to be clear – I don't blame the church. It would be too easy to do that. Blaming others, people and institutions, is quite the norm these days. I do not wish to play this blame game. The church, initially, assisted me in hearing and obeying the directive God issued to me. Remember, the A.M.E. Zion Book of Discipline lays it out that we recognize "those gifts and graces requisite to the proper and faithful discharge of the duties of the Christian ministry."[10] The church accepted and celebrated that when I answered this call that I had or desired some integrity that meant I was "moved upon by the Holy Ghost to preach." When I answered this call and said yes to God, the church acknowledged (or at least assumed) that I had "right judgment in the things of God." In other words, no one doubted that I had indeed heard the call of God; in fact, it is probably the case with many of us that some wondered what took us so long to answer this call! There were people in our lives who believed they knew God was calling us before we acknowledged it or recognized it, and they prodded us to heed that call.

---

[10] *2000 A.M.E. Zion Book of Discipline*, Qualifications and Rules for a Preacher, p. 73, par. 188

The question now seems to be whether or not something has skewered this once "right judgment." Where I was once clear about my aims in answering to that first "yes" when I responded to the call to preach, I have discovered that the systems of the church do not always support its aims. So like Adam, I found "fig leaves" of my own choosing to hide the fact that I am naked before God and must confess that I have not been true to the first "yes" to which I responded – the real reason that I answered the call to preach. That first "yes" was that call I answered to **PREACH**.

Now the great need and burning desire for me, and I am sure for other preachers as well, is to get back on track. Other persons, misguided notions and selfish or uninformed agendas cannot, or at least should not, ultimately decide what one hears from God and how we respond and say "yes" to God's call on our lives. This acceptance of the call to preach must come from the heart, soul and spirit of the individual who has heard clearly the voice of God from within the confines of their own heart.

Here again, we meet a potentially dangerous complication if there is any conflict about that "yes" we offered to God. People are willing to give to preachers and pastors in many cases authority in the church. Members of the church are willing to give to pastors this kind of control in large part because of the traditional understanding of what a pastor is or is supposed to do. The minister is deemed to have some special connection with God, so the people trust that person to understand things that the "average" member or parishioner will not. How interesting it is, then, that in the ordination of preachers, the bishop gives this directive: "Take thou authority…to preach the Word of God…"[11] It is important to note that when we are ordained, we are told to take authority – not responsibility. It is my belief that preachers take responsibility for too many things in the church. I suggest that I don't need to take responsibility for the church because since the church is the Bride of Christ, the church already has a husband. Our ordination suggests, in fact insists, that we instead take authority. We seem to take many things in the church, but authority is often, unfortunately,

[11] *2000 A.M.E. Zion Book of Discipline,* The Form of Ordaining Elders, p. 375

not one of them. When the prophet Isaiah and Jesus himself proclaim, "The Spirit of the Lord is on me" (Luke 4:18), they both declare with authority that the Spirit is given for a specific reason, and it is directly related to proclamation and preaching, the very thing to which we gave our first "yes." We have been anointed to "preach good news to the poor…proclaim freedom for the prisoners and recovery of sight for the blind, to release the oppressed, to proclaim the year of the Lord's favor" (Luke 4:18-19). In responding to and reclaiming that first yes, we will find again the most significant thing we do in our role as ministers of the gospel is to proclaim the good news – good news to the captives that they can be released, good news to the blind that they receive sight, good news to the oppressed that they go free, and good news to all that need to hear it that this is the year their deliverance is possible because it is the year of the Lord's favor – in other words, that the time for their salvation is now!

I like to watch *The Daily Show with Jon Stewart* each night before I go to bed. I am convinced of the wisdom of Proverbs 17:22, that "A cheerful heart is good medicine," so I try to make sure I enjoy a good laugh before I go to sleep. On an episode of the show a few years ago, former President Jimmy Carter was the guest. He was on the show promoting his book, *Our Endangered Values: America's Moral Crisis.* In the friendly banter he shared with the host, President Carter clearly exuded a confidence and sense of inner peace that comes from a man who has clearly tapped into what really matters in his life. Discussing topics from teaching Sunday school in his home church to building houses for Habitat for Humanity, President Carter clearly knows what he wants to do with his life. I took particular notice of this because President Carter has been the focus of a great deal of criticism and even scorn since he left the office of the presidency (and a fair amount of criticism while he held the office) from people who disagree with him, and who often use their own megaphone to express that disagreement. But Jimmy Carter is clearly comfortable in his own skin.

This comfort President Carter exuded was inspiring to me, and while I thought I knew its source, I wanted to probe it deeper. I started thinking about the first "yes" I said to God, which began for me (in terms of ministry) on July 16, 1975. I remember that on the night of my trial sermon the text was from the text Acts 9:6 (KJV): "And he trembling and astonished said, 'Lord, what wilt thou have me to do?' And the Lord said unto him, 'Arise, and go into the city, and it shall be told thee what thou must do.'" Now, some more than 30 years later, I think I am beginning to understand what that first "yes" would mean for me. The journey began that night had a seed which God planted and would later grow, nurtured by a powerful truth that was contained for me in this trial sermon text I chose: "Lord, what wilt thou have me to do?" It is a question that continues to be asked and an answer that continues to unfold in my life. No, I did not fully understand what my saying "yes" meant on that day as I began the journey. But I had to start; I had heard the call of God upon my life, and there was no resisting, and there is still no reneging, at least not if fulfillment is going to ever be found. And in the years since as have I journeyed with God, my heart and mind full of question like the one that the text in Acts 9:6 was prompting me to ask, I kept discovering, kept rejoicing, kept feeling inspired by and am always amazed at God's wonderful way of answering my first "yes" with a "Yes" from Him that predated mine by an eternity that traces back to Creation. And I have found that in every crisis, in every trial, with every joy and each victory, the words of Annie Johnson Flint affirm my testimony:

He giveth more grace as our burdens
grow greater
He sendeth more strength as
our labors increase;
To added afflictions He addeth His mercy
To multiplied trials He multiplies peace.

When we have exhausted our store
of endurance
When our strength has failed ere the day
is half done;
When we reach the end of our
hoarded resources
Our Father's full giving is only begun.

Fear not that thy need shall exceed
His provision
Our God ever yearns His resources to share;
Lean hard on the arm everlasting, availing
The Father both thee and thy load will upbear.
His love has no limits, His grace
has no measure
His power no boundary known unto men;
For out of His infinite riches in Jesus
He giveth, and giveth, and giveth again.

If as preachers you have any questions lingering in your heart or mind about what your "yes" means or meant, I would like to suggest that you go back to the trial or initial sermon you preached, examine that text again, and see if there is something God was saying to you then that will now make sense in a larger, broader, more significant way than you could have ever imagined when you began your journey with Him by saying "yes" the first time. And I would be willing to venture a guess that God is still speaking to you, and in fact calling you to say "yes" again.

CHAPTER 3

THE IMPORTANT VS. THE IMPERATIVE

> One way to think about one's leadership role is to ask the question, 'What is it for which the church looks to me which, if I do not do it, no one else can or will? Another way to ask this is, 'What is it that the church has a right to expect of me? What is it that, if I do not do it, no one else will because they do not have either the position or the preparation to do it?[12]

You can cause a good deal of trouble in your life by making one monumental

[12] Lovett H. Weems, Jr., *Church Leadership; Vision, Team, Culture and Integrity*, Abingdon Press, 1993. P. 27

decision: that you will define yourself rather than allow others to define you.

It is curious how people around you will react to that decision. You will be called names like "arrogant" or "stuck-up" and "know it all." You will hear people say of you, "He thinks he's all that" or "She has her nose up in the air." For sure, you will attract your share of "haters."

But try to remember something: people never "hate on you" when they are in agreement with you! When people like you or agree with you, then you are "decisive," "determined" and "full of conviction" and "know how to take charge." It's all a matter of perception.

Be very clear about what you are going to do with your life and ministry, particularly if you are a pastor, because when you are not, I promise you, there will be all too many people lining up to tell you what you should do. It may be that the reason we have so much confusion about what ministry and preaching are and what pastors are supposed to do is that we have allowed so many people to register their opinions on what the definition is and offer their own definitions, so that we pastors and preachers now are faced with some difficulty knowing what we are really supposed to be and do. Unfortunately, many of the persons chiming in to make their views known have not the faintest idea of what the definition of your ministry should be, nor what parameters should define it. When it comes to definitions of ministry, preaching and the call to pastor, we know what we know and don't seem terribly interested in finding out what we don't know.

I gather there must have been a time in the not too distant past when the main thing that a preacher was supposed to do was preach. That almost sounds too simple, and maybe that was how we got off track. Someone floated the idea in our culture that preachers don't do much except on Sundays. Others had "important" work to do, things more significant – or so it seemed – and all the preacher had to do was to fill an hour and a half or two hours on a Sunday and then he was done; how hard could that be?

The trouble began when preachers began buying this description of ourselves and started finding "important" work to do – as if anything could be more important than preaching God's word to a dying world.

This same scenario was presented once to a group of pastors. We read about it in Acts 6. They had formed a ministerial alliance of sorts –they were known as "the Twelve" (Acts 6:2). Now certainly there were things that needed to be done – the church was growing, people were hungry, widows were being neglected, and because there was so much to do it meant that some persons were being overlooked and even possibly ignored. And we know that no one likes being *ignored*.

What intrigues me about reading this story in the book of Acts is how the apostles handled this situation. Maybe they realized that how they handled this would set the tone for the definition of their ministerial function. What is clear is that they did not feel that it was necessary for them to add yet another responsibility to their already full schedules. They had quite enough to do. Their agendas were full because they gave their attention to "prayer and the ministry of the word" (Acts 6:4). They offered no apologies for this, they did not try to make themselves feel or seem more important by engaging in "busy work" – they stayed at the task to which they believed they were called, the tasks of prayer and the ministry of the word.

They had to feel pretty secure about themselves to tell those who wanted to load their day with other responsibilities "Thanks, but no thanks, that's not my job." I mean they risked being called lazy, shiftless or laggards by the people who were doing "important" work in the community. They might even have heard the whispers from those who suggested that they get a "real job." Imagine how their kids must have felt on Career Day at school when all the other dads came discussing how busy and involved their day was, doing this and fixing that and correcting the other, while Peter Jr. wants to crawl under his desk while his dad says, "Well, I used to be a fisherman, but quit that job about three years ago to follow a man named Jesus. Now I spend my whole day thinking about what he said and taught so I can tell others about it." I'm telling you, you can cause a good deal of trouble in your life if you decide to define yourself rather than allow others to define you.

But you know, I think those twelve apostles in Acts 6 got it right. They knew that they had the highest calling and the greatest responsibility that anyone could ever have, to preach the gospel. I have bristled at the suggestion by some that I "don't have anything to do" when they examine what they believe to be my life and work, since "all I have to do is preach on Sundays." But these twelve apostles are such an inspiration to me. They understood the difference between the "important" and the "imperative" and they were not going to let those who did not understand the difference mess it up for them.

So let's define the difference. There are important things that need to be done in the church. I mean, somebody has to "run" the church, right? And since we in the modern church have so carefully cultivated the notion that lay people or those not of the clergy are somehow not as capable or qualified as we professionals, the preachers, well, who else is going to do it? There are meetings to attend, committees to appoint, decisions to be made, funds to be raised, people to impress, and the list goes on. Those are important things, and yes, they need to be done. But this begs the question: who should do those important things?

In Acts 6 it appears that the apostles were clear that these important things were not their responsibility to do, and so they refused to do it. "It would not be right for us to neglect the ministry of the word of God in order to wait on tables (Acts 6:2). This should not be understood to say that if the apostles did not undertake this work themselves that it was therefore in their eyes not important work to be done. This is an important point to cite because very often the argument made for why pastors must attend this meeting or that function is because the presence of the pastor or preacher gives weight and potency to the event. No, the apostles were simply saying that this important work was not theirs to do, and if they neglected the work they were called to do, then the imperative work that is their chief responsibility will suffer as a result. So they gave the instructions to the multitude that they should "choose seven men from among you who are known to be full of the Spirit and wisdom. We will turn this responsibility over to them" (Acts 6:3).

This is going out on a limb, but I am making an appeal that we release our pastors and preachers from the burdensome task of being at every anniversary tea, club meeting and gathering of people that the local church or larger denomination now requires. Having to be present at all these occasions ultimately hurts the cause of the integrity of preaching. The place and time, preachers, when your presence is most important – I would suggest imperative – and most needed is on Sunday when you stand to preach to a congregation of people waiting to hear "what thus says the Lord." The church deemed that the preaching of God's word is an indispensible part of the worship. Be clear here – I am not making an argument for the personality of the pastor/preacher. I am saying that

God's word is paramount as a part of the revelation that unfolds in a worship setting. It may take some courage to do it, but it might be worth the risk to learn that many in your congregation would sacrifice your presence at the functions to which you thought yourself indispensible if it meant that you could spend a little more time in the presence of God, seeking God's revelation for the word you are responsible to preach.

Now, I can remember so well being told that I should never allow an officer in my church to tell me that "I can just preach and they will run the church" and that I should be outraged that anyone would even dare to make such a suggestion. That would be considered an insult of the highest order, a belittling of my station as a preacher and pastor. Some pastors might even remove an officer from his or her position on the spot for daring to voice such an idea. It has taken me a few years, but I now understand that I should not have been insulted by such a request. Now I imagine how liberating it would be to free myself from all these responsibilities that have nothing to do with the thing I believed in my heart I was saying "yes" to when I answered the call that God placed on my life. When I said "yes" it meant to me that I would preach God's word; I keep thinking about how much more fruitful my ministry could be if I could devote the time and energy that I have been diverting to going to meeting after meeting, attending to some church business, putting out fires and solving problems and addressing a crisis, when the call upon my life is the call to prayer and the study of the word. There is no reason that I should feel offended if the laity wants to run the church. In fact, I should encourage them to do so. It is my job, according to Ephesians 4:12 (NRSV), is to "equip the saints for the work of ministry, for building up the body of Christ" and not, as the apostles asserted in Acts 6:2, to "wait at tables," in other words, to do things that others could do just as well, but that I do not allow, either because of tradition or fear. I interpret these passages to mean that there are specific responsibilities given to those who answer the call to the Christian preaching ministry and other responsibilities given to other members of the body of Christ. So my challenge now is to back away from anything that does not relate to what I first promised God I would do, which is to preach the gospel. There are other areas of ministry and service that can be done just as well by others with adequate gifts, and I can be free to be true to the responsibility of preaching, which is the call that I answered from God and to which I said my first "yes."

Remembering what that first "yes" was and why you said it is vital to keeping us grounded. If we forget what that first "yes" was all about and why it was given, we start to think that we are more important to the scheme of things than we really are, and more importantly, we lose focus and perspective. Instead of being insulted if someone suggests that I spend my time preaching while they "run the church" I will celebrate that opportunity. Sometimes when people think they are insulting you, they are in fact helping you and doing you a favor; their words may bring you back to your senses.

The Biblical character David had such a moment. When he tried to bring the ark of God back to Jerusalem, his efforts were at first unsuccessful. The oxen that carried the ark stumbled, a man named Uzza, who was probably well meaning but misguided tried to steady the ark to keep it from falling, and as a result he died. David was at a loss for what he should do. He was so disheartened by the prospect of ever getting the ark back that he appears to have given up, until he realized that the ark, which symbolized the presence of God, was the cause of the blessing that fell in the house of a man by the name of Obed-Edom. Now David followed the instructions for transporting the ark down to the last detail and the ark was brought back to Jerusalem.

As a result of meeting with this success, David rejoiced, so much so that "David danced before the Lord with all his might" (2 Samuel 6:14). This scene did not set well with David's wife, Michal, and we are told she "despised him in her heart." Perhaps meaning to insult or belittle him, she said to him (2 Samuel 6:20), "How the king of Israel has distinguished himself today, disrobing in the sight of the slave girls of his servants as any vulgar fellow would!" This is one of those moments when David might have been insulted; he was being told he was not acting like a king would act, but rather he was acting like a shepherd, and in fact, it was embarrassing. It must have been one of the jarring moments of revelation for David. I'd like to think that in the words of his wife Michal, he heard again the call to which he first said "yes." He did not first say "yes" the call to be a king, his first "yes" and primary responsibility was to the task of being a shepherd. Perhaps he took this as a welcome reminder of what his main function in the world was to be, as indicated by his response in v. 21: "It was before the Lord, who chose me rather than your father or anyone from his house when he appointed me ruler over the Lord's people Israel — I will celebrate before the Lord."

This is indeed a challenge that we must accept. We must rediscover, reshape and redefine the meaning of our ministries so that all will clearly understand that we did not say "yes" to

God so that we could be a political mover and shaker, either in the denomination or my local community. I did not say "yes" to preach so that I could be a "personality" or a "star" in the church system. I did not say "yes" to preach so that I could manage the corporation called the church. It is frightening to think or to realize that some may have come to the ranks of ministry for that reason. They will have to give an account for themselves on that, but that was not my motivation. In fact, no one stands before any sanctioning body to receive the authority the church grants to one who desires or expresses a call to preach and suggests any other intention than that of preaching God's word. I said "yes" to God with that desire in my heart and mind. What I have discovered is that something has transpired in the course of my living out what I thought I was called to do, so that now other issues, other things and other concerns have somehow taken center stage. I am engaged far too much in the important and neglecting the imperative. As I and other pastors and preachers continue to do this, our ministries are placed in jeopardy. We must get back to that first "yes." This has led me to think in new and different ways about the leadership that I am called and expected to provide, and what the church expects of me.

We need to seriously consider what it is that we seek when we enter the preaching ministry, and say "yes." What compelled us to respond to this call? Did we seek affirmation in ways that we could not find in other venues of life? Was this call of God, like the call of God on the lives of several Old Testament prophets, so irresistible that we could not avoid saying "yes" though we tried? There certainly are compelling - and sometimes bad - reasons one may enter the ministry, which is why these questions must be examined and re-examined from a perspective of truth so that hopefully we will not continue as individuals in denial if our initial reasons for saying "yes" were not honest and forthright. If some secret, hidden agenda pushed us to a "yes," we must acknowledge that and correct our course.

I do not deny that such a course correction will be difficult, especially if I discover or admit, as Eugene Peterson acknowledged, that "all the models I had were either managerial or messianic."[13] This is not meant as a gratuitous swipe at my predecessors or leaders. There are, to be sure, good and not so good role models in every generation. I am, as I cited earlier, partial to the model set forth in Ephesians 4:11-13 as the ideal for pastors because it clearly sets forth a useful paradigm for the ministry of the pastor. It should be our goal to hold high such an example for those in our congregations and those following us in the ministry so that their "yes" when answering God's call will be honest and well founded.

In my own experience, anecdotal to be sure, I have found that many of my colleagues are of the opinion that the meetings which pastors are

[13] Eugene H. Peterson, *Under the Unpredictable Plant,* Wm. B. Eerdmans Publishing, Grand Rapids, 1992 p.27

expected to attend are fruitless and counterproductive to what we should be doing as pastors. As I indicated earlier, we are expected to attend these meetings because it justifies someone's idea of leadership. When pressed for a reason, the only explanation given seems to be that pastors have to attend these meetings because people expect us to lead, and this is part of our leadership responsibility. And, as often happens when people are uncooperative, when appeals to our conscience don't work, then guilt is the next tactic employed. We are told that the people are looking to us for leadership and support, and that the congregations and leaders of these meetings expect the pastors to show up, and so it is implied that you are derelict in your duty if you do not. Finally, when appeals and guilt don't work, threats usually follow. Some of our leaders have suggested gently or stated implicitly that our appointments as pastors are in jeopardy or the cooperation of the members in the pew will subside or disappear if we do not support these endeavors. If you have a family to support and a mortgage to pay, this is not a risk that you will take without grave consideration.

I admit that I don't understand this. I fail to see the connection between attending meetings and church functions and my effectiveness in leading the people of God in a way that "equips the saints for ministry," much less is true to the first "yes" to which I promised God I would be faithful. Far too often, we as pastors are asked to prop up someone's idea of what a minister is or should be, and that idea is not consistent with what I read in Scripture or what I believe I should be doing. I am not appointing myself to be the spokesperson for pastors nor am I seeking to take on the role of champion for this cause; I am just asking that we reexamine the reasons for which we are involved, and in some cases, forcing responsibility to an idea that is leading to frustration and even burn-out in the ranks of our ministry.

Obviously, the simplest way to correct what is wrong is to ask ourselves what we are doing in ministry that someone else could quite easily do (and maybe even do better than we can), and then STOP DOING IT. Do only do the things that no one but you can do. In other words, do only what is imperative, and leave the important for someone else. This seems so elementary, so obvious that I frankly wonder why I did not think of this sooner in my ministry. Gordon MacDonald points out, rightly, I think, "Many Christian leaders will candidly admit they spend up to 80 percent of their time doing things at which they are second best."[14]

He warns us that the great danger of this is that "unseized time will flow in the direction of one's relative weakness,"[15] which is to say that those of us who are weak in administrative gifts (or if not weak in those areas, certainly it is not to that area of ministry that we gave our first "yes") will find that those concerns tend to swallow up our valuable time. How many of us

[14] Gordon MacDonald, *Ordering Your Private World,* Thomas Nelson Publishers, Nashville, 1984, P. 75
[15] Ibid., p.75

find that when it comes to sermon preparation, teaching and the things we need to do to "equip the saints" that we are woefully short on time because our time is consumed with going to meetings, putting out church fires, and attending to the business of the church, which in fact, someone else may be more equipped and gifted to do than we? We as pastors are simply going to have to make a commitment to redirect our time and energies toward those areas to which we first said "yes." It cannot be a justifiable argument when our preaching and teaching of God's Word is suffering, as in some cases it clearly is, to advocate for the presence of the pastor or preacher to attend a meeting, essentially to "wait on tables."

True, this may be easier said than done. Ronald E. Osborn, quoting sociologist Samuel W. Blizzard, cites

> The tasks the minister believes are most important and most enjoys doing are valued least by the people and are crowded out of the minister's week, whereas the tasks the minister regards as least significant and likes least are those by which the congregation measures success or failure and which eat up most of the time.[16]

Why is this easier said than done? Have we lost the sense of what is imperative, what is absolutely vital in ministry? I hope not, and I think not, but clearly I will have to make some choices. But I must agree with MacDonald:

> Sometimes I find such choices hard to make, simply because I like people to approve of me. When a person learns to

[16] Ronald E. Osborn, *Creative Disarray: Models of Ministry in a Changing America,* Chalice Press, 1991. P. 4

> say no to good things, he runs the risk of making enemies and making critics; and who needs more of those? So I find it hard to say no.[17]

What is interesting as we think about what MacDonald points out is that we pride ourselves in being independent and acting so. I know I have often said, "No one tells me what to do!" You know, I actually thought that was true until I took a closer look at my life and realized that I was strongly governed by the desire to please. I was trying to please church superiors, church members, and the status quo. But as I took a closer look at what I believe I promised God when I said "yes," I discovered I was in fact attempting to please the status quo or some

[17] Gordon MacDonald, *Ordering Your Private World,* Thomas Nelson Publishers, Nashville, 1984, p. 83

superior or authority and that now pleasing the status quo no longer felt good for me. I knew I needed to change, and realized, with some fear, that it would cost.

However, if we commit to doing only the imperative and leave the important tasks to someone else, it will give our ministry and our efforts focus. This is the lesson that Jethro gave Moses in Exodus 18:13-27. In verse 18, Jethro says to Moses, "You and these people who come to you will only wear yourselves out. The work is too heavy for you; you cannot handle it alone." The point that Jethro wisely made to Moses is that it is impossible to do too many tasks well. In fact, if we do, not only we but also the work we claim to care for suffers. We have a generation of ministers who are worn out, burned out and stressed out because we are doing things that we are at some deep level unhappy about doing. Something deep within tells us this is not what we said "yes" to in the first place.

Now this realization and taking a stand on this issue could cause difficulty for us pastors, especially if we stop doing things people expect us to do. It may be frightening to think about the many things that will be left undone if we commit to only what will "equip the saints for the work of the ministry" and do the work specifically to which we believe we are called. But we may also discover that perhaps our fears are unfounded.

> The apostles faced this temptation during the early stages of church life. A dispute arose in the church in Jerusalem because the Greek-speaking widows thought they were being slighted in

> the daily distribution of the food. This problem was laid at the apostles' feet. Here was an opportunity for the apostles to act as true servants and model care to the whole church. But the apostles decided that serving tables was not their primary call. They rightly saw this ministry opportunity as a diversion from their call to preach the word and to pray. "It is not right that we should neglect the word of God in order to wait on tables" (Acts 6:2). They refused to do so, not because it was beneath their dignity but because it was not their God-assigned call. To the extent that they refused to take on what was not theirs, they expanded ministry opportunities for others.[18]

When we allow ourselves to be drawn to the important and away from the imperative, we end up doing what is merely incidental. I believe that we should make every effort to avoid the

[18] Greg Ogden, *The Discipleship Malaise: Getting to the Root Cause,* The Journal of the American Academy of Ministry, Winter-Spring, 2003, Vol. 8, No. 2, p.7-8; ed., Jonathan Kever

incidental in our lives and ministries so that we can concentrate on the imperative. By incidental, I mean those things that just happen to become our responsibility because either no one else will do it, or we think no one else will do it as well. It will probably be shocking to pastors if they were to evaluate their time and examine how much of what consumes their day is what they absolutely have to do as opposed to what people expect them to do or have decided that they should do; we might likely discover they we are being stuck with jobs and responsibilities we don't want and don't enjoy in the first place. Many pastors fall into this category for a long time, believing (falsely) that they are the "straw that stirs the drink" as Reggie Jackson was once famously quoted as saying about himself when he came to New York to play baseball for the New York Yankees. This attitude leads to what C. Peter Wagner calls "the myth of the omnicompetent pastor." Wagner observes,

> An outmoded view of the pastor's role, although diminishing, strongly persists in some circles today. It is the view that the pastor is hired by the congregation to do all the ministry of the church. The better the pastor, the more the people of the church can relax and become spectators. It is not only an outmoded view, it is also unbiblical.[19]

If we need courage to do this (and we may), we can find a way out of this morass by looking again at the ritual of our ordination – and I start there because I am convinced that we must remind ourselves again and again what we

[19] C. Peter Wagner, *Your Spiritual Gifts Can Help Your Church Grow,* Regal Books, Ventura, CA, 1979. P. 133

promised to do. It is there, in those words that I am reminded of what I promised God on my knees that I would do. It would be well for us to read the service of ordination every so often so that we may remind ourselves of what we are all about. For that matter, our congregations should read it as well so that they will not make any unreasonable demands of us. It will save us all a great deal of frustration. We need seriously to ask if the direction in which the church is going is truly the direction in which the Holy Spirit is leading. Where the Holy Spirit will lead, He will need leaders to take the church in that direction, and if we are distracted by many other concerns and diverted from our primary calling, it will cause the church to suffer from misguided concerns and myopic focus. We should allow for the possibility that we have veered off course because we have listened to the voices of "traditions" and not the voice of the Holy Spirit. There can be no greater tragedy.

There is a Chinese proverb that says, "The beginning of wisdom is to call things by their right names." Pastors and preachers need the right definition to do the right job. So let me suggest something radical, maybe even a little crazy. Pastors, take a month, three months or six months off from going to any meetings. Get immersed in God's word for the people you lead and serve. Make the focus of your time preparing to preach and teach, to that which you said "yes" in the beginning. You will probably have some withdrawal symptoms, especially if you have conditioned or convinced yourself and the congregation to believe that these things are "important." But you might also discover, and they will too, that such things as have occupied and consumed your time away from God's word are not, and never were "imperative," that the church can do quite well without it and that we will all benefit from pastors and leaders who understand their true calling and answer only to that first "yes."

Chapter 4

Apostolic Movement or Administrative Management?

When pastors are asked about what they enjoy most about their job, teaching and preaching top the list. It's little wonder: Most of them believe they have the spiritual gift of teaching or preaching, and most of them spent a number of years in seminary honing their abilities of exegeting the Bible and communicating its truths.[20]

I use the words "apostle" and "apostolic" very carefully. These words have become

[20] George Barna, *The Second Coming of the Church,* Word Publishing, Nashville, TN, 1998. P. 36

associated in our present day with denominations and in some cases with persons who may have individually applied the title of "apostle" to themselves. Churches or individuals that use the term have perhaps anecdotally identify apostles as "a man (and they are almost always men) who has had a personal vision of, or encounter with Jesus Christ." The Scriptural example or model used to support this in the such churches has been the Apostle Paul, who referred to himself in 1 Corinthians 15:8 (NKJV) as an apostle "born out of due time." We may debate (and perhaps have reason to believe) that the use of this term "apostle" is a justification for giving one a title that seems to confer some special favor, gifts or anointing upon the one so called.

However, as we discussed earlier, for anyone who acknowledges the call to preach the gospel it is believed that he or she will evidence that call by means both "internal and external."[21] How can anyone assess or critique if one has had a "personal vision of or encounter with Jesus Christ" except by standards to be judged externally? Any examining committee such as the law of the A.M.E. Zion Church mandates at the District and Annual Conference level, for example, is in fact left with no other recourse but to take that person's word for the experience they claimed to have had. However, Methodism does not dispense licenses or ordinations based on such subjective testimony.

---

[21] *2000 A.M.E. Zion Book of Discipline,* Qualifications and Rules for a Preacher, p. 73, par. 188

The debate continues as to the use of the word "apostle." The New Unger's Bible Dictionary defines apostle as: "The official name of those twelve of the disciples chosen by our Lord to be with Him during His ministry and to whom He entrusted the organization of His church." This definition would suggest that the term apostle may not be applied to ministers or used by ministers today since

> As regards the apostolic office, it seems to have been preeminently that of founding the churches and upholding them by supernatural power specially bestowed for that purpose. It ceased, as a matter of course, with its first holders, all continuation of it, from the very conditions of its existence (cf. 1 Corinthians 9:1), being impossible. The bishops of the ancient churches coexisted with, and did not in any sense succeed, the apostles, and when it is claimed for bishops or any church officers that they are their

> successors it can be understood only chronologically and not officially.[22]

I recognize the difficulty here as the A.M.E. Zion Church, of which I am a member, has not recognized any such office or status as that of apostle. The Fausett's Bible Dictionary allows that the word apostle may also carry an expanded meaning or implication, but offers this caution:

Apostle is used in a vaguer sense of messengers of the churches (2 Corinthians 8:23; Philippians 2:25). But the term belongs in its stricter sense to the twelve alone; they alone were apostles of Christ. Their distinctive note is,

[22] *The New Unger's Bible Dictionary* from the PC Study Bible, Copyright 1993-1999, 3.0 Version for Windows

they were commissioned immediately by Jesus Himself.[23]

My purpose in raising this point is to engage in a different if not new discussion of how we see ministry in the church. We have surely read and are familiar with Matthew 16:16, where Peter makes his great confession of Jesus that "You are the Christ, the Son of the living God." In response to this declaration, Jesus says, "Blessed are you, Simon Bar-Jonah, for flesh and blood has not revealed this to you, but My Father who is in heaven. And I also say to you that you are Peter, and on this rock I will build My church, and the gates of Hades shall not prevail against it." I wish to raise the point

[23] *The Fausett's Bible Dictionary*, from the PC Study Bible, Copyright 1993-1999, 3.0 Version for Windows

here that I do not believe that this "authority" spoken of by the Lord Jesus was intended for Peter alone. Peter is described as the "rock" or the foundation on which the Church is built (in terms of his belief and faith), but it seems that it was never intended that he was to be the sole recipient of this power. This being the case, in churches that allow for the use or office of apostles, or that believe in "apostolic succession," our understanding of this term must broaden. We would have to argue for "apostolic succession" for all who believe in the power that the Holy Spirit gives, so that for everyone who is a believer it will be understood "that whatever you bind on earth shall be bound in heaven, and whatever you loose on earth will be loosed in heaven" (Matthew 16:19).

This should not require a great stretch, either theologically or logistically or in regard to church polity and practice. Thus I want to use the words "apostle" and "apostolic" to suggest that many modern day churches, particularly the A.ME. Zion Church, was established by persons who could rightly be called "apostles." For if the role of an apostle is "preeminently that of founding the churches and upholding them by supernatural power specially bestowed for that purpose" as defined by the New Ungers Bible Dictionary, then the organizers of many of our present day denominations, certainly those of the A.M.E. Zion Church, fit the definition of an apostle. The persons identified in Scripture as apostles were not unlike our leaders today:

> Shortly after their ordination 'He gave to them authority over unclean spirits, to cast them out, and to heal every kind of disease and every kind of sickness'... He gave to them authority over unclean spirits, to cast them out, and to heal every kind of disease and every kind of sickness. Jesus taught them to understand the spiritual meaning of His parables (Mark 4:10-34; Luke 8:9-18), and yet when He was removed from the earth their knowledge of His kingdom was limited (Luke 24:21; John 16:12).[24]

For what church or to which leader of the church could not these words be applied today?

My argument is that the church needs to retrace its apostolic beginnings. What we read in the Scriptures about apostles is that they were daring, they were willing to take risks for the sake of moving the people of God in new directions and to fresh places as the Spirit of God

[24] Ibid.

would lead them. William Jacob Walls, who served the A.M.E. Zion Church as a bishop for 50 years, would seem to argue for the apostolic role of our founders when he writes,

> In the formation of any organization that gains potency, there is practically always one who provides inspirational leadership and directional prudence, who is heavily depended upon by others to steer the ship sailing into new harbors, safely into port.[25]

Those persons who birthed the churches in which we worship and celebrate today did so in the face of what could have been disastrous consequences, and are to be commended for their courage. They were willing to face scorn, opposition and ridicule for a principle they

[25] William Jacob Walls, *Reality of the Black Church,* A.M.E. Zion Publishing House, Charlotte, NC, 1974. P. 44

held, in some cases religious freedom, in other cases social justice. There is little doubt that if the mindset of those persons who engineered the apostolic movement of the church in its origins had been that of "playing it safe" – an attitude we often find today and with which we are sadly comfortable – then it is doubtful, perhaps that we would have the benefits of worship we enjoy in our present time.

I suggest the biblical example of 1 Corinthians 12:28 as our guide, which says, "And God has appointed these in the church: *first apostles* (emphasis mine), second prophets, third teachers, after that miracles, then gifts of healings, helps, administrations, varieties of tongues." I believe it is important to understand why apostles are first in this order. As we have indicated, the apostles are risk takers, they lead the way, refusing to play it safe, and they are not afraid to blaze new trails for the church. Apostles are people guided by vision. George Barna explains that vision is

> A clear, mental image of a preferable future imparted by God to His chosen servants and is based upon an accurate understanding of God, self and circumstances...Vision is a picture held in your mind's eye of the way things could or should be in the days ahead.[26]

The church always needs and should always have apostles, people of vision, who will move the church into fresh places. That is what apostles and apostolic ministry does, it moves the church forward with new vision. This great

[26] George Barna, *The Power of Vision,* Regal Books, Ventura, CA. P.28-29

need which each generation has and for which each generation yearns forces us to ask: who are and where are the apostles in the church today? Is there anyone who is willing to take risks in our church, anyone who will go out on a limb and do something daring in response to that first "yes" that you heard?

Much is made and there is so much discussion from both leaders and lay alike about "tradition." No question, the traditions of our churches are rich. There are traditions the church celebrates and guards of which we are rightly proud. But while tradition is good and a worthy guidepost for our journey, sadly there are many who use the excuse of tradition to keep from having to do anything innovative. Tradition has in many instances ceased being a marker and has now become a roadblock. If nothing else moves us to make innovative changes, the fact that the world is changing and leaving the church behind as a nearly dying relic of the past should motivate us to take action, and quickly.

Without question, the world has changed around us. The culture around us is not going to wait or care if we notice. To make this point, I usually cite an example from my childhood and the church in which I grew up, Mother A.M.E. Zion Church in New York City, or more specifically, Harlem. As a child growing up in the church, I had lots of friends in the church. All around 137th Street, located in the heart of Harlem, there were children from all over the neighborhood that attended the church. My closest friends in church were Kevin, Tyrone,

William and Herbert, and all of them lived on the block where the church is or at least within walking distance of the church. My family lived in the Bronx, about a half an hour ride away on the train. However, we maintained our membership at Mother Zion because it was the family church. The idea of moving our membership was apparently never considered by my family.

Mother A.M.E. Zion Church in the days of my youth had a neighborhood from which to draw. Houses and apartments were available and occupied on that street and throughout the surrounding neighborhood and the adjoining streets from which perspective members could be encouraged to attend. That is not the case any longer. The community that once surrounded Mother Zion has seriously deteriorated and is now all but gone. And thus Mother Zion has endured the fate of many inner city churches. For one thing, it is the case that people no longer as a rule go to the "neighborhood church" as was the case in my childhood. The average person does not feel compelled to go to that church closest to home as they once did or may have. People are more inclined to find a church that "meets their needs." Some will argue that "meeting the needs" of people is too arbitrary a standard by which to grow a church or build people in faith. This may be true, but there is another factor that must also be considered. The fact is that whether or not we like it or are willing to admit it, denominational loyalty is on the decline. This is due, at least in part, to the fact that

> The vast majority of mainline congregations find themselves on a numerical plateau, trying to relate to the diversity of tastes and opinions both within the church and in the surrounding community.[27]

Statistics, empirical data and experience may all tell us how true the factors of decline are, but in many conversations you hear or engage in with some of our leaders and members today, you will be met with an insistence that nothing at all is wrong. Only in what we sometimes refer to as the "outdoor committees" at meetings do you hear statements to the contrary to what is said in the public spaces of the church. It is the case, sadly, that

[27] E. Stanley Ott, "*Twelve Dynamic Shifts for Transforming Your Church,* Eerdmans, Grand Rapids, 2002. P. 4

> Because churches are nonprofit entities whose existence requires only a name and a person or two to maintain the legacy, a dead church is not necessarily an ex-church...As long as these churches have a handful of faithful attenders and can afford some meeting space and a speaker, they remain in existence.[28]

These facts may mean that some of our "traditions" will prove the death knell for our churches. The traditions we are seeking to preserve are sometimes not held or kept for the benefit of those we hope to reach; they are preserved rather in the interest of those who are presently members, because "we've always done it this way." So we must ask a difficult question when we look at our churches, "Who is our client?"[29]

---

[28] George Barna, *Turn Around Churches,* Regal Books, Ventura, CA, 1993. P. 22-23
[29] Lyle Schaller, *Strategies for Change,* Abingdon Press, 1993 P. 25

We may then discover that the client we seek to serve is the existing membership, not the masses we declare comprise the center and focus of our interest as we seek to fulfill the mandate of the Lord Jesus in the Great Commission, to "Go and make disciples of all nations, baptizing them in the name of the Father and of the Son and of the Holy Spirit."

Let me be clear: by no means do I want to question the value or importance of tradition, nor do I want to suggest that the so-called "traditional" church has no place in our society and ecclesiastical circles today. In fact, I wish we could put to rest these arguments that consume us about the competing value of the "traditional" versus the "contemporary" church. I agree with E. Stanley Ott, who suggests, a traditional church "may be vital if they are building disciples and meeting people's needs."[30] The question that should guide us as we look at the means of our ministry is probably best phrased by the advice that television personality Dr. Phil has often given on his television show: "How's that working for you?" Rather than expending so much energy on which model is better, let's examine which models work and use them, and after making our appraisal, discard the models that don't. The goal of the church is to make disciples; whenever our methods fail to do that, those methods should be abandoned, since our goal should be to please our Lord, and not ourselves. In other

[30] E. Stanley Ott, *Twelve Dynamic Shifts for Transforming Your Church,* Wm. B. Eerdmans Publishing, Grand Rapids, 2002. P. 13

words, if what we are doing is not working, if our efforts are not accomplishing the goal of making disciples, then those methods should be abandoned because they are not true to God's purpose for the church.

Each generation and each church as it reflects on its own history will find its share of persons rightly designated as apostles whose dedication and labor has blessed the church by their commitment and influence. If there are any traditions that we should emulate, it should be those traditions that grow the church, not shrink the church down to a size that is manageable for our control. In the A.M.E. Zion Church, I would cite as apostles in our history stalwarts such as Bishop Thomas H. Lomax, Bishop J.W. Hood, and Bishop J.J. Clinton, each of whom moved Zion furth

the East Coast. We

Talbot Jones as well

Home and Foreign

Missionary Society.

from in my lifetime ... and expansionist vision of the late Bishop Herbert Bell Shaw, who expanded the borders of the A.M.E. Zion Church to England, Jamaica, Trinidad-Tobago and revived the work in the Bahamas Islands; Bishop George J. Leake, who took the A.M.E. Zion Church to the "Last Frontier" in the state of Alaska; and Bishop Richard Laymon Fisher, who lengthened the borders of Zion to include an Annual Conference in the state of Arizona. These men and women set the example we should follow, one seeks to grow the church and of its members. All too often it be the agenda of many leaders at all ...s of the church to make the work comfortable for their needs, not the concerns of the Kingdom. The history of the A.M.E. Zion Church will show that other new Annual Conferences have been established by bishops of our church in recent years, but those Conferences have been established primarily overseas, and that is why I do not cite them here. I am focusing on the home land of North America for arguments about apostolic work, since, as William Easum states that among the new paradigm shifts that we will have to accept is that "North America is the new mission field."[31] I wonder

[31] William Easum, *"Dancing With Dinosaurs: Ministry in a Hostile and Hurting World,* Abingdon Press, Nashville,

if we have become content to do nothing more than to maintain the vision and efforts of these giants of the past. If so, it should be disturbing, and clearly the results for the church will not be favorable.

In this passage we cited from 1 Corinthians 12, we must take note that farther down the list of gifts that God gives the church is the gift of administration. It may be that today's church is operating ineffectively and our ministries are futile and fruitless because we are looking to administrators to do the work of apostles. What is the difference between administrators and apostles? Administrators tend to only maintain what the apostles gave birth to through

1993. P. 13

prayer and vision. This is because the focus of an administrator is order, method and regulation. Administrators are usually not willing to risk anything. Administrators are not pioneers; they are concerned with playing it safe.

I do not dismiss the work of the administrator; there is a place for bureaucracy in any organization, but bureaucracy should not be the guiding force of a ministry. Bureaucracy limits the emphasis of leadership in the church to one of management and makes the primary issue one of control. The greatest detriment is reflected in what Jim Collins highlights in his book, *Good to Great*, where Collins observes,

> The purpose of a bureaucracy is to compensate for incompetence and lack of discipline – a problem that largely goes away if you have the right people in the first place. Most companies (churches)

> build their bureaucratic rules to manage the small percentage of wrong people on the bus, which in turn drives away the right people on the bus, which increases the need for more bureaucracy to compensate for incompetence and lack of discipline, which further drives the right people away.[32]

When ministry in the church becomes largely a function of bureaucracy, the result is that organization and administration then become the church's primary gifts. Now, the traditionalists are not totally wrong. Organization is always necessary; God is not the author of confusion and disorder (1 Corinthians 14:33). Administration is necessary as there must be direction for the thrust of ministry efforts. To be sure, there are some traditions that we have in

[32] Jim Collins, *Good to Great,* Harper Business, 2001. P. 121

the church that we must preserve because they tell us who we are, where we have come from, and they give us our stable foundation; I will say more about this later. This is exactly the role that traditions are designed to play in any life, group or entity. But the error of those who seek to preserve some traditions is that they may be failing to understand or realize that not all traditions deserve to be maintained. Some have served their purpose and should be allowed to fade out. Those concerned only about tradition may fail to realize what in the church needs to be preserved and what needs to be given a decent burial. They may be too short-sighted to understand that change is happening around us whether we like it and whether we accept it or not. It is to our disadvantage to ignore this because "when any organization decided it will seek to save its life by building walls against change, that organization is destined to lose its life and its vitality."[33]

An example I often like to cite concerns people who work with computers, either at home or in their workplace. Every time I suggest this scenario, I get an almost violent reaction: suppose you returned home or to your job to discover that someone had removed all the latest computer technology and replaced that equipment with manual typewriters because they wanted to preserve "tradition?" The reaction is never favorable; in fact, I can see that if such a situation was to be enacted, the exodus

[33] Lovett H. Weems, Jr., *Church Leadership: Vision, Team, Culture and Integrity,* Abingdon Press, Nashville, p. 39

would be so hurried it would leave your head spinning! So it appears we may be stuck in a prison of our own making:

> Learned ignorance is a crutch that some people use. They deliberately appear ignorant or helpless when they are not. They think the same way they've always thought or think the same way people around them think because it's easier than thinking for themselves. Learned ignorance…is the refusal to take full accountability and responsibility for your life. It means preferring to remain ignorant about something because, "If I'm ignorant, I cannot be held responsible.[34]

This is why I suggest that as preachers, we must return to our ordination vows; we have been ordained first to word, then to sacrament and then finally to order. It is this to which we gave our first "yes." We have inverted this

[34] Vashti Murphy McKenzie, *Journey to the Well: 12 Lessons on Personal Transformation,* Penguin Compass, 2002. P. 113

sequence; we have flipped the script. We have made our ministry focus order, sacrament and word. The face of our ministry would change immediately if we focused less on administrative management and more on apostolic movement. It seems now to be a radical suggestion, but preachers should discover again that to which we gave assent when we answered the call to preach. Ministry is supposed to be rewarding and often is, but it can be a frustrating task as well. Let's be honest, it is true and somewhat frightening that more and more we find ministers are suffering from the deleterious effects of the frustrating aspects of ministry. Ministers are increasingly experiencing "burn out" - which Wikipedia defines as "a psychological term for the experience of long-term exhaustion and diminished interest." Doesn't it seem contradictory and odd that the God we preach as the God of all supply and comfort, the One who said, "Come to me, all you that are weary and burdened and I will give you rest" would permit us to be so frustrated from exhaustion and diminished interest?

It is so tragic that so many in ministry are in this predicament because if asked it is likely that most pastors will acknowledge that the areas where we are called to spend the majority of our time and in the areas which end up consuming our concerns (administrative management) are not the areas where we feel we are most gifted or truly called to serve the church (apostolic movement). This is a tension which increases with the responsibility of becoming what many regard a "first church pastor." There is a troubling element of being a pastor so described: are the leading pastors in our church regarded as being the premier preachers of their community and even among their peers? Are the persons selected for these leading pulpits chosen by the leadership of the church for their exegetical skill in rightly dividing the Word? Unfortunately, the feeling exists (granted, because it is a feeling this is anecdotal and may in some cases be an unfair assessment to make) that very often such factors as preaching ability and devotion and commitment to the first "yes" are not considered as strongly as other factors. It isn't likely that anyone in a position to make appointments (i.e., a bishop of the church) is outright going to *say* that persons are selected for reasons other than preaching skill and ability to lead a congregation spiritually; but the feeling of skepticism among the members in the pews as well as among some preachers is that other factors do come into play - payback, the "old boy's network," and even nepotism. Even if this idea was created out of a sense of professional or personal jealousy, if it in any degree applies, to continue this cycle will certainly spell doom. But doom does not have to be the end result for us. We can make a turn around and shift again the focus of our ministry in the direction of the apostolic.

I was inspired a few years ago to personally renew my commitment to the apostolic focus of my ministry when I visited San Diego, California, for the Mid-Winter meeting of the Christian Education Department of our church.

Arriving early for the meeting and with time to spare, I went with Rashad Smith, one of the youth of our church to Sea World in San Diego. We had a good time, but one particular venue made a great impact on me. We went to an exhibit for the manatee, an aquatic animal that is now categorized as an endangered species. I frankly wasn't terribly interested in the manatee, really kind of walking almost aimlessly through the exhibit as it was on our way through the Sea World park. But upon leaving the exhibit, there was a mural which carried this message: "Extinction is forever. Endangered means we still have time."

What a powerful message that held and still holds for me. Yes, we still have time. We have time to recapture the apostolic beginnings of our ministry, the part of us that heard God clearly when we answered the call to preach. We have time to be the preachers God meant for us to become. We have time to reclaim our ministries from the pull of the culture and the devastating effects of anything other than what God has in mind. We still have time to say "yes" again.

I truly love ministry. I love how I have the opportunity to serve people. I love how my gifts put me in the place where people come expectantly to the church in anticipation of what God has given me to give to them through His word. I find no greater joy in life than to see the look on the faces of the members whose lives have been transformed, changed, redirected or encouraged because I am in the moment of our interaction, the instrument of God. I try to be careful simply to stay in touch with the needs of the people, and to relish the joy of knowing that those needs are being met by the way that God uses me. I am continually moved by the honor and trust people bestow upon me, so touched by the confidence they place in me, so overwhelmed by the faith they have in me, and I want to live up to that expectation, for them, but most of all, for the God to whom I first said "yes." I am grateful and thank God that the privilege has been mine to try to be what a pastor is supposed to be and do. This is why when I am called away to administrative duties in the community or to functions of my office in the District or the Conference or the Connection, I want to try to remember this. There are those moments of apostolic power that I am blessed and anointed to know when I stand to preach and answer that "yes" I gave back in 1975, the opportunity to minister in the way that Jesus would have his ministers to share with the flock of God. I do believe that members understand that pastors are busy and that sometimes duties call us away. But nothing, absolutely nothing, can or should replace the sole and primary responsibility of dispensing God's word to God's people. And I pray that we will never seek to find a substitute.

Chapter 5

Striving for Significance rather than Success

Our souls are not hungry for fame, comfort, wealth, or power. Those rewards create almost as many problems as they solve. Our souls are hungry for meaning, for the sense that we have figured out how to live so that our lives matter, so that the world will be at least a little bit different for our having passed through it.[35]

It is the love of preaching that brings me to this task. I am saddened to see that so many of my colleagues have left this which was once

[35] Harold S. Kushner, *When All You've Ever Wanted Isn't Enough,* Pocket Books, New York, 1986. P. 18

the first love. I am disappointed to discover that so many of our churches and the people who occupy the pews have no appreciation for the importance of preaching. If I could wave a magic wand, the rediscovery of the paramount place of preaching would be immediate.

I acknowledge that some have left this primary work because for them the expectations of ministry were becoming tedious. Something had to be sacrificed and that something became preaching. Because our lives are so finite, the fact is that it is possible to say "yes" effectively to only one thing at a time. When the demands are too great, something must be sacrificed, and that something became preaching. For several friends, in the desire to fulfill what was their call, leaving the denomination (the A.M.E. Zion

Church) and the ranks of pastoral ministry was the best option. Some were overwhelmed by the demands of their superiors, others felt constrained by the lack of freedom to move in the Spirit as they felt led, while others felt a desire for something new and fresh and different in their ministry which they felt that the denomination and its structure did not provide or support. Some left the denomination altogether, others just moved into other areas of ministry other than the pastorate. I have been tempted to consider some of these options as well, but realized that an impulsive move in any direction would not solve the problem that I faced. What I needed was clarity for my ministry. It seemed that the only way I could achieve that goal was to find again the original focus of my ministry, the first "yes."

In the search to recover that yes, I discovered another problem, and it is one that I notice confronts many preachers, to a greater or lesser degree. It is the desire to be perceived a success. The measure of what that means is broad, and at the root of the problem is an unclear definition of what success in ministry will look like, therefore making the picture ever more unclear.

Too much of what will pass for success has been determined by our culture. The number of people who fill the pews, the amount of money raised in the offerings, the status of the pastor in the denominational circles, the clout she carries in the community with the movers and shakers have now become important factors, more important, sadly, than how much time one spends immersed in the Word of God so that the people who come to the pews will hear from God whom they seek on Sunday morning.

Now, admittedly, it is really quite difficult to make this point because you almost can't make it without admitting to being at least tempted, if not flattered and enticed by the very evil you decry. I have come to see that there is a "reward system" firmly in place in the church – in every church system, and we are all very aware of it. And in many cases we have, or want to, benefit from that reward system. The church's recognition, commendation, approbation and remunerations are things that we all seek to a greater or lesser degree, whether or not we openly admit it. Very often, it seems that appointments are made and positions are considered based on this system of rewards. Some of what makes and keeps this reward system in place is the sense of entitlement that is found in the church.

I find this sense of entitlement sad. There is rightfully no place for a discussion of what one "deserves" in ministry. To engage in such conversation is proof of how far we have drifted from that first "yes." By what logic have we come to the right to feel that we are entitled to anything? This attitude is the very antithesis of the gospel we preach, and it must be snatched up by its root and discarded, cast out and put to rout. Christian ministry is about service. It is not supposed to be about how lucrative your "package" is that the church can provide. That criteria misses the point entirely.

When I was appointed to Memorial A.M.E. Zion Church in Rochester, New York, the most frequent comment that I heard was, "Congratulations. You deserve it." Finally, I said to someone who made the comment to me, "No, I don't. No one deserves to go to Memorial." Now, of course, I know what they meant to convey, the idea that I had done my work, had been faithful to my task as a pastor and this was the culmination of my labor that was reaping its proper harvest. But the question I found myself raising was, does anyone "deserve" to be the pastor at Memorial, or the pastor of any church for that matter? Is it not more likely that, as I once heard Dr. Andre Resner say, that ministry is not "have to" but rather "get to?" I am not, and should not consider myself to be where

I am because I have worked my way up the ranks, as if on some corporate ladder. This is the core attitude that breeds much of the bitterness that exists in ministry today, where preachers of all rank and station are angry and disappointed because they do not get the appointment they "deserve." We should rather see ourselves as where we are in ministry because God by grace has opened doors for us to utilize the gifts God has made available to those of us willing to serve. That would mean that I would apply the gifts given to me with the same desire, interest, intensity and devotion no matter the size, scale, salary or significance of the church, because I realize that what I do I do for God, not for the recognition of my peers or superiors in the hope of gaining some benefit or reward or the trappings of success.

This is the reason I have never wanted to subscribe to the idea of being the pastor of a "small" church. That is, I believe, a dangerous idea for the church to foster, an even more egregious notion for a preacher of the gospel to embrace. We do not serve a small God, so how do we come to the idea that some churches are "small?" To speak of a church being a small church, we are speaking in relation to the *size* of the membership. It then leads to this idea of small churches that is infectious to the *attitude* of the membership and the leadership. I am convinced that every church has (or should have) a reason for being, a reason to exist. And if we believe that God has placed each of us in the church with various and diverse gifts, there is room in the Body of Christ for the pastor whose gifts will be appropriate for the church with 100 members or less. That means that the size or number of a congregation is not a value statement about the effectiveness or significance of a church. Of course, what makes it difficult to appreciate this is our constant yearning for advancement and the endless chase for this elusive idea of "success." This is perhaps how we have reached the unfortunate place in ministry where "what started out as managing people's gifts for the work of the kingdom of God becomes the manipulation of people's lives for the building up of my pastoral ego."[36]

[36] Eugene H. Peterson, *Under the Unpredictable Plant,* Wm. B. Eerdmans Publishing, Grand Rapids, 1992, p.181

So, how do we rate success? If success for you looks like popularity, I want to guarantee you right now that you are going to be disappointed. Some people by nature are quite competitive and they will make it their life's work to "bring you down a peg" if they think you are getting "too big for your britches." In other words, when you are making advancements in your field, even in the field of ministry, you are going to have your share of "haters." It's a fact; deal with it. No one is going to be liked by everybody. I remember hearing Bill Cosby say that he never knew the key to success but he was sure that the key to failure was trying to please everybody. If you are a leader and you make decisions you are bound to make people mad. If you are infected with the "need to please" you will surely not do anything that will rock the boat and that will pretty much insure that you are going to be at the mercy of people and their fickle desires for you. There has to be a better way to do what we feel we are in fact called to do.

A closer look at Exodus 2:11-14 will help us understand how the quest for popularity and acceptance is futile. In that well known passage Moses kills an Egyptian who was beating one of his fellow Hebrews. I for one had never noticed the obvious – if Moses in fact, as the text indicates, "looked this way and that" before killing the Egyptian, and "seeing no one killed the Egyptian and hid him in the sand," then who is the person who speaks to Moses the next day when Moses steps in to settle a disagreement between two Hebrews? Apparently, it is the person whom Moses rescued the previous day, who having been rescued from the danger now past, turns now to Moses and says, "Who made you ruler and judge over us? Are you thinking of killing me as you killed the Egyptian?" (Exodus 2:14). Moses ends up being resented by the very person he was trying to save! That can be a very frustrating reality to face, but it may be one that many of us in ministry have indeed had to confront, especially when we want or seek popularity and success.

We all know too many preachers and pastors who measure their success by the size of their church congregation, salary, prestige and profile among his or her colleagues. That standard is fine for the world; clearly our culture revolves around fame and money, which is why the highest paid persons in our society are sports figures and entertainers. This cannot be the gauge by which we measure our ministry or the church. The biggest problem I see with the way some pastors at some of the so-called "smaller" appointments do ministry is that they appear to or are failing to realize that the church with 15, or 150 members deserves quality in ministry as well as the church with 1500 or 15,000 members - and not just to do such a good job at the church with 15 members so that you can get the attention of the bishop and move to the larger appointment of 150 or 1500 members. This of course is a vicious cycle, because if you do well, you are promoted and you get recognition and more of the reward systems benefits that the church is all too willing to provide. My point is that the promotion should never be the goal for ministry.

I am not living in a fantasy world, I hope, but I think that many preachers are like I was. When I started out preaching in 1975, I was so just glad to preach! I would preach anytime, anywhere, and many times I went at my own expense, never being reimbursed, and had to bring my own congregation - my mother, grandmother, and my three best friends, Robbie, Ronnie and David. I realize that our needs change (now we have families to support, for example) but I don't want to lose that preacher that I knew in 1975, because that preacher wanted nothing more than to preach and be faithful to the gospel. How well I am committed and dedicated to the function of ministry should be for us the real definition of success in ministry.

At the end of the day, our core values will determine the way we do our ministry. I'm suggesting we should focus instead on what is *significant* in our ministries rather than what may pass for *success*. In other words, we must concentrate on what we are doing that makes a difference to the people to whom we minister. Never mind these ephemeral rewards that the world and even the church have to offer. I want it to be said of me what was said of David in Acts 13:36: "David had served God's purpose in his own generation…" Success is too fleeting a standard to apply to a labor that should have eternal value.

The standard or the measurement we call success is something that is largely conferred on us, and it comes to us from a criterion that is imposed on us by someone else's idea or paradigm of what success is, and this is precisely why success is dangerous. Sooner or later we will all discover that if someone has the power to build you up, they have just as much power to tear you down. If someone or something else can define success for you, that person or that thing will become god to you. Jesus gives us the perfect model for ministry because he was clear about his definition of himself, and he knew exactly what he came to do (Mark 1:35-38) and that is what Jesus did. We must never lose sight of why we are sent in the first place, that to which we first said "yes" when we answered God's call.

In a world and in the church where our priorities are so confused and mixed up, we need to change the situation by asking a different question, which is a key role for leadership. Someone must have the courage to ask different questions about how ministry is conducted in our day and in our church. Of course, it may be risky to do this. Those who dare to make this kind of inquiry must face their demons. The question that we should ask is why am I in ministry now? Better yet, and even more piercing, why did I go into the ministry in the first place? Did I really hear the voice of God calling me to a task which I found irresistible because I knew this was what I was supposed to do with my life, or did I get into this because I was attempting to please someone, or even myself, rather than God? We may fear asking these questions in dread of the answers we will discover, but to not ask these questions means that we will continue to be untrue to the church that sanctioned us and gave us authority which in the long run we will ultimately abuse. To be sure these questions challenge us, but in fact such questions reverberate in our minds week after week, if there is any sense of true calling on our lives. But we must not fear these questions because we are called to be change agents. Anyone with absolutely no talent or vision at all can do what the previous generation had done. But the people who make the greatest difference in any situation are the people who dare risking being different.

The question then should not be how I can be successful in ministry. The question should be, what difference does it make that I answered the call of God for my life? Is the church different, better, empowered, more enlightened because I answered God's summons? Has my ministry made a difference at all? And with that question, we need to ask by what criteria do we measure that difference? If success is defined by the minister with the highest profile in the church or community, or the largest appointment or accoutrements that go along with the trappings of success, then for such success, the minister has difficulty finding definition in line with what should be that first "yes."

It is disturbing to some of us that our ministries have lost focus. In our great concern and push for what passes for success, we have lost our way. Here is a significant danger here of which we must be aware. I try to remain aware of this by remembering some advice given to me by a pastor at that time in Charlotte, North Carolina, Dr. George E. Battle, Jr., who is now my bishop. As I began my pastoral journey, he was invited to be the guest lecturer for the Hood Seminary retreat one year while I was a student in the Master of Divinity program. I had been assigned to the church at Clarkton, North Carolina, Pierce Chapel A.M.E. Zion Church, and I was unsure of myself in this situation and I wanted nothing more than to be a "success." But I wasn't sure how to go about it, or how to make that happen. So I asked Dr. Battle for advice on how to pastor this church. And the advice he gave me still applies in any ministry situation I face even now. He said to me, "Just love the people." This advice bodes well for me in each appointment I have held, and it is sagacious advice for every preacher who would assume the responsibility to lead the people of God. We are, from the moment we receive the ordination to ministry, and again when we receive our first appointment and each succeeding appointment from the hand of a bishop to be a shepherd in the church of Jesus Christ, accountable to God for the way we lead God's people, and it still holds true that the best and most effective way to lead these people is with love.

It is imperative for the church that we figure out, sooner rather than later, that nothing else will bring us happiness or accomplish for us the sense of success we so desperately crave than to do that which we call ministry God's way. Ultimately, leadership in the church is significantly and primarily a spiritual endeavor. It is not, and should not, be measured by acumen or insight by any calculation, no matter how impressive it may be. The intoxicating results of having the kind of power that makes people and issues move has infected the church all the way down to the rank and file. I am convinced it is responsible in large measure for nearly ruining the church as we know it today.

Success cannot even be about "getting things done" if in the getting things done it is not consistent with the first "yes." I notice that when I, as a pastor, want something done in my church, it is up to me to persuade and inspire, to convince and motivate the people I lead to cooperate with the vision or suggestion that I have put forth. The further we go in ministry – if, for example we are blessed to enjoy a long pastorate at one church, and particularly, it seems, when one reaches a status of advanced leadership in the church (i.e., a bishop) – it seems we are less inclined to feel compelled to persuade or motivate. We treat ministry as though the best and most effective way to get things done is to demand it. We conduct ministry much the way a fraternity does a hazing ritual – we understand the insanity of it, but we don't seem very interested in correcting what is clearly bad behavior. The unfortunate result is that we are perpetuating this bad behavior for the generations to come.

How badly are we missing the point? To illustrate, let's take a story from the gospel of Mark where we find a disturbing tale. In the ninth chapter of his gospel, Mark tells us that the disciples of Jesus were unable to cast out of a young boy a demon which possessed him. It is embarrassing and disappointing that the father of this young boy approaches Jesus and says with perhaps a mixture of sadness or disgust, "Teacher, I brought you my son, who is possessed by a spirit that has robbed him of speech. Whenever it seizes him, it throws him to the ground. He foams at the mouth, gnashes his teeth and becomes rigid. I asked your disciples to drive out the spirit, but they could not" (Mark 9:17-18).

The drama deepens and the situation worsens. These same disciples who were unable to cast out the demon, found themselves engaged in an argument on their way home about which of them is the greatest (v. 33-34). I'm guessing this question would quite easily have been answered if any of them had enough power to cast out the demon from the boy.

Then, as if to drive home the point of their complete misdirection of purpose, the disciples then inform Jesus "Teacher, we saw a man driving out demons in your name and we told him to stop, because he was not one of us" (Mark 9:38).

So, let's see – the disciples are unable to cast a demon out of a boy, they engage in a pointless and internecine argument about which of them was the greatest, and then they chastise someone who they find doing what they are unable to do.

They have managed in one fell swoop to prove to us the absurdity of seeking success instead of significance in ministry, and worse, they have managed to show that when you go after success without being significant – that is, making a difference in the lives of people to whom you minister – you end up with neither success nor significance as the legacy left behind. The disciples were rendered completely irrelevant to the situation of the boy who was demon possessed, they were unsuccessful in the task of ministry immediately before them, and in the wake of their fruitless ministry and inapposite endeavors no one is helped and they are left arguing about things that have no consequence whatsoever. Of course, if we have no power to do what we are supposed to do, then perhaps it is understandable why such distractions will occupy our time.

Returning to the first "yes" of our ministry will force us to abandon some of these windmill chasing, quixotic pursuits which consume so much of our time and energy. We, as ministers of the gospel must be clear about what it is that we are doing and supposed to do. If there is one lesson that I have learned and try to be cognizant of in my life, it is that when you are not sure of what to do in any situation, you will never be short of counselors with advice for how you ought to handle the matter. I am continually amazed, even astounded, at the number of people who are sure that they know what I am supposed to do as a pastor or minister. I don't want to be wholly critical of that, because there is value in counsel when it comes from the right person. But we ought to question at every turn why some people want to mold us into some image that is not consistent with what we believe we are called to do, in line with the gifts that God has given to each of us (1 Corinthians 12:4-7). Lovett Weems, Jr., comments,

> It is amazing how people so often make decisions and plan for the future out of faulty assumptions and

> mythology. This will often come out in statements such as, "When Pastor Smith was here...," or "We used to have more children than we could handle...," or "We need more space..."[37]

Weems further points out that "People never have enough information to make objective judgments based on reality. People must depend on the perceptions they receive from the culture to make their judgments and decisions."[38]

I always have thought it would be most interesting and helpful to find out how people initially received this former pastor who is now such a hero to the congregation while he or she served the congregation. People being people,

[37] Lovett H. Weems, Jr., *Church Leadership: Vision, Team, Culture and Integrity,* Abingdon Press, Nashville, P. 51
[38] Ibid., p. 119

in all likelihood, they rejected those ideas and vision as well, at least for a time.

I urge and remind myself and my colleagues in ministry to stay focused, to be clear and sure about the task at hand, to be certain with as much certainty as possible that I am answering that first "yes" that initiated the call of God on my life. Because we are unsure or misguided about what it is that God has called us to do, ministry has become the wrong kind of burden. William H. Willimon shares the advice that he received from an older preacher when trying to figure out if he was in fact called to preach: "Don't even try being a pastor unless you are called, unless you have no way of avoiding the summons."[39]

The unfortunate result of our recent relentless pursuit of success in the church, in my lifetime and experience, has been that we have not only lost our way, we have lost our identity. We no longer know who we are, and as such we are subject to the definitions of others who have no sense of what it is that the minister is supposed to do with his or her life as a person called by God. That is not the way I believe it was meant to be. It certainly is a difficult process to discover for ourselves what it means to be called of God, to answer and live out that call in its fullest meaning. For anyone truly called of God, from

[39] William H. Willimon, *Pastor: The Theology and Practice of Ordained Ministry,* Abingdon Press, Nashville, 2002. P. 51

the days of the prophets and sages of Scripture until the present, the wrestling and struggle for definition and clarity of what this call means has gripped us as we seek to be true to what it is that God wants from us. It seems, however, that the answer continues to be the same: the call on the life of a man or woman is not a call to success, fame, notoriety, celebrity or renown. The call is to be faithful, even unto death, as Revelation 2:10 admonishes: "Be faithful even to the point of death, and I will give you the crown of life."

This is for me now a deep conviction of my heart. I am truly concerned that I maintain the integrity of my ministry and that I do not lose my true purpose in this quest for what some define as success. If I put my life and my ministry and the call God has placed upon my life in the hands of arbitrary and capricious men and women, it is inevitable that I will be hurt and disappointed. It is just this simple – if people have the power to make you, they will also have the power to break you. And the list of people that have been broken and hurt by the whim or quirk of individuals, yes, even in the church, is too long to include in any body of work. We have to trust again that God will see and reward our faithfulness if we will be faithful to do what we are called to do. I want to believe that my time will come and that a measure of success will come in the way that God would have it, without my seeking it brazenly. I find encouragement and support for this idea from the beginning of the ministry of a young prophet named Elisha.

Elisha's mentor, the prophet Elijah, was a great and monumental figure in the history of Israel. He blazes on the scene with the impressive and extraordinary announcement that it will not rain again until he gives the word (1 Kings 17:1). With that, he promptly disappears from the scene. Elijah is portrayed as fearless, bold and audacious when speaking the word of the Lord. But he is also all too human, "a man just like us" (James 5:17) and as such, we are not shielded from seeing his faults and disappointments. At once intrepid and valiant, he is also seen as vacillating and unsure when he receives the threat from Jezebel that he will be killed in the same fashion as he killed the prophets of Baal (1 Kings 19:2). He runs away in disappointment and fear at hearing this. Under a juniper tree in the wilderness, Elijah throws himself a pity party, saying to God (1 Kings 19:4), "I have had enough, Lord," he said. "Take my life; I am no better than my ancestors."

This story resonates with me because in seeking to recover the integrity of what I understood as the call upon my life to preach, I want to be very careful not to be arrogant and high-minded. There is a compelling temptation to look across the landscape of the church and at others in ministry and decide that no one has it right but me. In part out of frustration and in part because one can indeed be sincerely devoted to what is understood to be God's revealed will, we can become impatient with others and think that they are woefully off track and that they need "me" to help set them straight. Indeed, it may be part of my role is to set things right, as Paul instructed his young protégé Titus to do in the city of Crete (Titus 1:5); when we see things that in our vision and understanding are wrong, we indeed have an obligation to seek to make it right. But when I get to the point that I think that the survival of the institution depends on me, I have moved into dangerous territory.

Elijah wants to change the world - a noble quest to be sure - but perhaps Elijah needed to deal with the intractable core from which he operated when doing what God called him to do. Seemingly possessed by what the *With the Word Bible Commentary* calls "the Elijah complex," the prophet Elijah has understood God to work in only one way, and is disappointed by the lack of God's cooperation with his plan.

It is likely this mentality that leads him to such great despair after such glowing victories and deciding that his ministry has suddenly become worthless and fruitless, and as such, the prophet pleads with God that he might die (1 Kings 19:4).

We should count ourselves fortunate that God does not acquiesce to our desires at times like this. Grace from God fortunately does not allow that in a pique or a tantrum I will be able to walk away from my call or my life because I have not achieved the success that I desired. It is not success, I am now reminded, to which I am called. So what, I hear God say, that you didn't get the appointment you wanted? So what, God tells me, you have been overlooked (in your estimation) *again*? So what if those whom you feel are less qualified or better connected are moving up the ranks of the church's corporate ladder faster than you? It is to none of these things that you have been called. That was not your first "yes." So in essence, what God gently (or maybe not so gently) says to Elijah, to you and to me is, "Get over yourself!." Elijah expects to find God in the spectacular displays of mountain splitting winds, earthquakes and fires, but God is not found in any of them. Finally, in the sound of "sheer silence" God is heard. Upon hearing God this time, Elijah is instructed to anoint two new kings and to install and anoint Elisha "to succeed you as prophet" (1 Kings 19:16). God sure knows how to put an out of control ego in place! Just when Elijah was beginning to believe that the world of prophetic utterance rested and revolved around him, God reminded him, "No, it doesn't. I have seven thousand servants you know nothing about who are faithful and loyal to me, and I can count on them even if I can't count on you."

And so Elijah sets out on his search for his successor. It is fascinating to me where this successor is found, and it is this passage that calls for humility and reminds me that success is not the goal. Elijah finds Elisha plowing a field. A humble task, to be sure. No great fanfare is attached to this endeavor. What is most significant is that the story finds Elisha "plowing with twelve yoke of oxen, and he himself was driving the twelfth pair" (I Kings 19:19). This is significant because Elisha was apparently not from a family of little means. One could make the case that Elisha probably did not even have to plow the field at all if his family had enough wealth to hire eleven workers – what hurt could hiring one more bring? But here he is plowing, and at that, plowing at the back of the line. And the story of the text finds Elisha working diligently and faithfully, perhaps even in relative obscurity, when the prophet who will become his mentor comes to find him and throws his mantle on his shoulder, and then walks away.

This is, to me, a powerful example of how we should trust that God will affect his call upon our lives, and that when the time comes for that to happen, nothing can avert God's plan. Our task and challenge is to be faithful and diligent in our tasks, even if we operate in those tasks without the notice and fanfare that we may desire and secretly seek. I do not believe that in our initial response to God's call, upon responding "yes" for the first time to the moving of the Holy Spirit upon our hearts, that we sought to respond so that we could become church celebrities. Even if we were impressed by the trappings of power and prominence such as the church may offer (and admittedly, it is hard to imagine that any of us, impressionable human beings that we are, could not have been awed by that at some level), I cannot help but believe that our greatest desire when we answered God's call was to do the will of God as best we understood it. I remember the thrill that I felt in my heart upon responding to God's call, and I did not see that response in light of any the definitions of success that I have discussed. I want to be faithful to the call of God and make a difference in the lives of the men, women, boys and girls to whom I am sent to share God's love and word. To do this, we must be constantly vigilant of our desires for that which will connect us to what may be deemed successful by anything other than the definition set by Jesus himself, because such success often comes at the expense of the sacrifice Christ calls us to make for the Kingdom, and remaining faithful to that first "yes."

CHAPTER 6

THE PASTOR AS PRIEST AND PROPHET.

Should there be any wonder about the boredom people suffer in church? A city goes wild with excitement over an athletic contest that is ultimately irrelevant except as a test of skill and spirit, but people go to sleep in church. Why? Because they see no contest there. Church leaders fear controversy like the plague; they want a pastor whom Joseph Sittler characterized 'a combination of master of ceremonies and soothing friend.' Such a minister may be "nice," but hardly exciting.[40]

There is a tension existent in the church. Perhaps it has always been there, and

[40] Ronald E. Osborn, *Creative Disarray: Models of Ministry in a Changing America,* Chalice Press, 1991, P. 193

perhaps will continue to be, but this tension is unnecessary. It is the tension that exists between the traditional and the contemporary. People, preachers and leaders have taken their positions on opposite sides of this dividing wall, quarreling with each other about which is more necessary for the church. The argument is pointless because it is possible, even necessary, that we understand that a pastor is both priest and prophet.

Among other detrimental results, this tension has created a sense of despair in the work of pastors, dissatisfaction with our responsibilities and perhaps even disgust with our vocation. This is most unfortunate. Work is redeeming and this is why we must pursue with renewed intensity the true work that God has called us as preachers to do. This is not to say that we have to enjoy our jobs (or the people we are called to work with) all time; no one I know enjoys their job all the time. There will always be people with whom we disagree, situations we do not like and events that we cannot control, even in the Lord's work. My point is that as pastors and ministers we must be clear about our meaning, purpose and definition for ministry. No one else should be allowed the responsibility to define us. That means that pretending, fitting in, conforming, or kowtowing to the desires of the status quo (particularly and especially when that status quo is not consistent with the first "yes") are no longer options for us.

I do not wish to convey the idea that this point of clarity will be arrived at with ease. In fact, the journey will be time consuming and sometimes tedious. It may create as many enemies as friends, as many adversaries as allies. There are going to be a number of people who will not, in fact, who cannot possibly understand what you are doing or trying to do.

> Most of us arrive at a sense of self and vocation only after a long journey through alien lands. But this journey bears no resemblance to the trouble-free "travel packages" sold by the tourism industry. It is more akin to the ancient tradition of pilgrimage – "a transformative journey to the sacred center' full of hardships, darkness and peril."[41]

You should prepare to risk being called uncomplimentary names behind your back and to have people treat you differently because they can no longer handle you. There are some in ministry, and perhaps there always will be, who desire nothing more for themselves or the churches they serve. They seem all too content

[41] Parker J. Palmer, *Let Your Life Speak,* Jossey-Bass, San Francisco, 2000. P. 17-18

to preach and live by a gospel of "just enough" – by that I mean they will do just enough to get to heaven or just enough to avoid hell. That is not, it seems to me, what Jesus calls us to enjoy in relationship with him. Does not Jesus in the gospel proclaim, "I came that they might have life, and have it abundantly" (John 10:10, NRSV)? Should not this promise extend to the realm of our ministries as well? Why should we settle for anything less?

And yet, so often we do, and worse, we subject the people we serve to our diminished vision and the distressing results. I challenge you to take the risk, let's embark on the journey to be the men and women God called us to be – people who answer to the true call, that first "yes" that will be the anchor as well as the rudder for our task. To be true to the call, throw caution to the wind - do what God demands of us! I know this all sounds frightening, but I steel my nerves and buck up my courage when I remember a favorite hymn:

"It may be in the valley where countless
dangers hide,
It may be in the sunshine where I
in peace abide,
But this one thing I know, if it be dark or fair,
If Jesus goes with me, I'll go anywhere."

So let us journey on. Let's look first at the role of the pastor as priest. My journey has brought me to an understanding and appreciation of what it means to be priest for the people I serve.

> I have never understood what it means to be a priest more clearly than I do now. People look to priests to be

> authentic witnesses to God's active role in the world, to his love. They don't want us to be politicians or business managers; they are not interested in the petty conflicts that may show up in parish or diocesan life. Instead, people simply want us to be with them in the joys and sorrows of their lives. I understand that organization is important. The Church as a human institution needs a certain amount of administration. But structures can take on a life of their own and obscure the real work with people that priests should be doing.[42]

This passage by Joseph Cardinal Bernardin explains as well as anything what ministry has become. It seems that we have become so consumed with the trappings of administration and function in the church that we now actually believe that the average person in the pew really cares about these mundane, trivial matters that

[42] Joseph Cardinal Bernardin, *The Gift of Peace,* Image Doubleday, New York. P. 89

consume us. Well, on second thought, they do, and that is also an indication of the misguided direction of ministry, that it is the widely held belief that it is the job of the minister to address these concerns. It would probably hurt the feelings of those who have seemingly given their lives so completely to this area of focus, but here's a news flash: what our members really want is a pastor who is there with them when they hurt, who will share their joys, participate in the daily grind that becomes their life, and will walk with them and be their friend and guide and spiritual counselor.

We must understand our role as priests, for as priests, we are the repositories as well as the dispensers of the church's traditions. To carry on the traditions of the church is a high honor and a great privilege. To do this faithfully, it is necessary that we know, understand, appreciate and convey the meaning of the church's rituals. A ritual is for the church a pattern of action. This pattern of action allows the church to maintain its uniqueness in a culture awash with confusion. Rituals are given and were established with the clear intent of teaching people the ways of God. Every time the church gathers, we gather to remember and be reminded who we are and what we are supposed to do in the world.

We are going to have to wrestle with the rituals of our church, with their theological significance, with their meaning and intent, and not just perform ritual mindlessly and without thinking about what these things mean and how they are intended to impact and guide our lives. For starters, I would suggest that we distinguish carefully between tradition and ritual in the church.

Now, I hope the distinction I want to assert will not be a source of confusion. I do not suggest that tradition and ritual are one and the same. The distinction I want to make in the use of these words may be difficult to prove except in practice. "Tradition" as the Webster's New World Dictionary defines it, is "the handing down orally of customs, beliefs, etc., from generation to generation." "Ritual" is defined as "of, like, or done as a rite (a ceremonial or solemn act, as in religious use)." In these definitions, one can begin to see the problem. Something we do or regard as a ritual is so designated because it is passed down through tradition. This forces us to ask: What in our churches is ritual, and what is merely tradition? What is absolutely, uniquely connected to the way we worship or who we are as a people, and what has just become habit or form that now we just find difficult to release?

Human beings are poor conveyors of messages that have to be repeated again and again. Do you remember playing the game "telephone" when you were a child? After a few times of telling what is supposed to be the same story, the story loses its originality, and before you know it, you end up with a story far different from the story with which you began. Do I mean to suggest by this argument that there is no value for tradition or ritual in the church? Not at all. But what I do mean to say is that unless there is careful and vigilant reexamination of the ritual and tradition, just like in the game of telephone, the story will get lost, and the truth and meaning behind the act vanishes.

An example - anecdotal, to be sure - is found in the experience of a friend, now a bishop in our church, Bishop Kenneth Monroe, who shared with me an interesting story. It had become a tradition, and perhaps closely associated with the ritual of the sacrament of Holy Communion on the first Sunday in the church where he was pastor (and in most churches, I might add) that the entire altar, including the altar rail where people kneel, would be covered in white. At some point, the question rose as to why this was done. When he asked the Deaconesses, who were responsible for preparing the altar for the sacrament why this was done, one Deaconess responded, "Because the pulpit is holy on the first Sundays." That response led him to ask, "Isn't the pulpit holy every Sunday?" The point here is that somehow, the dressing of the altar in white – tradition – had become confused and mixed up with the ritual – Holy Communion – and they were regarded as one and the same.

It is a very interesting exercise to draw the line between ritual and tradition in the church. There are things that every church does that have risen to the rank of ritual, things that are not necessarily wrong, but do not deserve such designation. They are merely tradition – a part of the church's culture, defined by Lovett Weems as "who we are and how we do things around here."[43] These may include such things as where people sit in the sanctuary (you have no idea how much trouble you can cause in some churches if you sit in the wrong pew!), and what Sunday a particular choir sings. It is an unspoken rule and understood fact that if a particular choir or group has sung on a particular Sunday for as long as anyone can remember only the most daring of pastors, and only after a long tenure at that same church, would dare to alter the pattern. While these are somewhat harmless and even bemusing examples, more serious damage is done when the significant traditions of our church are not observed or explained. Why, for example, does the choir process into the sanc-

[43] Lovett H. Weems, Jr., *Take the Next Step: Leading Lasting Change in the Church,* Abingdon Press, Nashville, p. 59

tuary with a particular type of hymn? What significance is there in sitting versus standing during prayer or reading Scripture? And who is responsible for answering such questions for the congregation locally, or the church as a denomination?

My answer would be that the pastor, the person designated as "priest" is the person who should do this. The knowledge that the parishioners gain about the meaning of the church's rituals is acquired through the understanding of the church's symbols, and it is the pastor's job to convey and explain this significance. Paul Tillich writes, "Man's ultimate concern must be expressed symbolically, because symbolic language alone is able to express the ultimate (as) symbols point beyond themselves to something else."[44]

Someone must chart the course and set the direction with clarity and lucidity which direction the church will go, and why. The pastor as priest must keep before the people the significance of the symbols we use. It is the pastor as priest who is the dispenser of the traditions of the church, and is responsible to also explain why those traditions are important, not merely to stand before the congregation and complain that they are not doing it well, or proclaim that there is no room for discussion about change because "this is the Methodist way" (or whatever denomination is at issue). It seems that

[44] Paul Tillich, *Dynamics of Faith,* HarperCollins Publishers, New York, 1957. P. 47

people need a better and sounder reason for doing what we do in worship and sacrament than the preacher or Presiding Elder or Bishop saying, "Because I said so."

This should all be of particular interest and concern to those who proclaim that they are interested in preserving the traditions of the church. There are great legacies of the church that must be carried on, that need to be kept alive for this generation and for generations to come. Sadly, many of the traditions of the church are dying a slow death, and the reason for this is not only that the younger generations do not appreciate them. The sad truth is that those traditions have not held meaning for those who have practiced them for a long time, they have become devoid of meaning and purpose, now done by many only by rote, habit and mere routine. Thus, Paul Tillich is correct when he observes, "Symbols do not grow because people are longing for them, and they do not die because of scientific or practical criticism. They die because they can no longer produce response in the group where they originally found expression."[45]

It is important that I understand my role as priest. In doing so, I can avoid the temptation the culture presents to be irrelevantly innovative. As Lovett Weems, Jr. observes, "Almost all new visions cross old bridges."[46] As priest, both for the local church where I serve and in the interest of the community that surrounds

---

[45] Ibid., p. 50

[46] Lovett H. Weems, Jr., *Take the Next Step: Leading Lasting Change in the Church,* Abingdon Press, Nashville, p. 67

me, I am called to remember that I am not an inventor of new knowledge. I am, rather, to be a faithful custodian of accumulated truth, story and behavior in the community called the church. This is why we do not need to fear tradition, and it is so sad that tradition has gotten a bad rap. Marva J. Dawn helps us with an important distinction when she writes,

> Much of the antipathy arises from a confusion between tradition and traditionalism. Historian Jaroslav Pelikan's brilliant distinction is forever apt that traditionalism is the dead faith of the living, whereas tradition is the living faith of the dead. In our churches' struggles over such issues as worship forms and styles, for example, traditionalism usually becomes an idolatry of "the way it's always been done." In contrast, to value the Church's tradition is to recognize that our forebears in the faith had many insights into what worship means, that their hymns and liturgies and symbols have carried the faith well, and that therefore those tools and forms are

> vital for immersing us in the presence of God...Both sides are wrong if they fail to ask the deeper, crucial question: How best do we hear and worship God? Since God probably has widely eclectic tastes and since God is vastly more than we could ever imagine, sufficiently describe, and worthily praise, certainly we need a vast array of musical sounds and worship forms to immerse us in a more adequate sense of all that he is![47]

Tradition is not imposing on us something that is restrictive and suffocating. In the pastor's role as priest, he/she carefully discriminates what from the past needs to be preserved, handed on and defended. There are some wonderful, glorious traditions of the church that we must guard with every fiber of our being as pastors. However we package it in our ministry,

[47] Marva J. Dawn and Eugene Peterson, *The Unnecessary Pastor: Rediscovering the Call,* Regent College Publishing, Vancouver, p. 35

every week in our preaching, we are saying, in the words of the hymn, "I love to tell the story, of unseen things above, Of Jesus and his glory, of Jesus and his love; I love to tell the story, because I know 'tis true, it satisfies my longing as nothing else can do. I love to tell the story, 'twill be my theme in glory, to tell the old, old story of Jesus and his love."

What our parishioners, and yes, even the world, needs to hear, is about that love that God wants to lavish on us. There is no need for people to come to church to hear the latest news; they can get that from any of the 24 hour news stations, the Internet or their local newspaper. Commentators and pundits and bloggers are now everywhere. It is nearly impossible to turn on your television anymore without hearing some "expert" on whatever the issue of the day happens to be. People are inundated with such information, and have the opportunity to hear all sides of every issue with the switch of the remote control. The message of God's love grounds the soul in a foundation that is sure, that will prove lasting when the shifting sands of culture and fad move the landscape where we have settled in. The man or woman who steps into the role of priest, who guards valuable tradition and serves as a dispenser of these beloved conventions, gives the people whom they serve a center from which to function and find meaning. There should not be a revolving door into and out of discipleship. The clear path that the priest marks in his or her ministry for those who would be followers of Jesus Christ is toward the Kingdom of God.

The mistake that I believe many have made, and continue to make, is in not understanding tradition's function and limits. Tradition is not intended to get us stuck where we are, neither is it supposed to be unable to move us into a new appreciation of what God is doing now. Sometimes we ought to ask: how long does it take for a phase to become a rut? There is certainly value in keeping the traditions of the past, but there also comes a time when you have to know when God is leading you to new and innovative positions. "Change," says Lovett Weems, Jr., "is not becoming something we have never been before. It is become more of what we have been."[48]

It is most significant and vital in light of this that the pastor have the ability to lead the church in making the transition properly. This is where the pastor's role as prophet comes in. The word and the image of the "prophet" evoke some images that are incorrect to the understanding of what God calls the prophet to do. The prophet speaks now and to some degree always has spoken against the background noise of, for example those who claim psychic powers or the ability to communicate with the dead. People who are desperate for answers will easily give

[48] Lovett H. Weems, Jr., . *Take the Next Step: Leading Lasting Change in the Church,* Abingdon Press, Nashville, p. 71

heed to these offers of false hope. The prophet has a different role and purpose:

> Almost every prophet brings consolation, promise, and the hope of reconciliation along with censure and castigation. He begins with *a message of doom*; he concludes with *a message of hope*. The prominent theme is exhortation, not mere prediction. While it is true that foretelling is an important ingredient and may serve as a sign of the prophet's authority…his essential task is to declare the word of God to the here and now; to disclose the future in order to illumine what is involved in the present.[49]

So when God wants to lead the people to new places and new terrain in their journey toward the kingdom, the prophet's voice is called for. This message that is given and the voice that will proclaim it must be endowed with a power that

[49] Abraham J. Heschel, *The Prophets,* Harper & Row, New York, 1962. P. 12

cannot come from the authority of the appointment of the bishop or governing body alone. Change is not something that is embraced easily by people. It seems absurd, but people can get locked into habits and patterns that are detrimental and often they are unwilling to change even when those habits and patterns are ruining their lives or deterring their forward progress.

This explains as well as anything the rut in which many churches and leaders fall, stuck in the way we've always done things, unable to release the past to see and enjoy a more profitable future. Of course, there must be a sure foundation on which to build the future of a life or organization. Success cannot be possible if a person or group is faddish, and changing merely to keep up with the Joneses. Yet we must also know when it is time to move on from the place that is no longer viable for us. In the life of the prophet Elijah, which we discussed earlier, there came a time for him when "the brook dried up" (1 Kings 17:7), when the place that once provided him water and refreshment became nothing more than a mud hole, and it was time to move on. It would have done Elijah little good to stay at what used to be the brook Cherith and reminisce about the way things used to be. This movement represents the journey that bridges the gap between the priestly and the prophetic.

This is the great challenge of leadership and what makes it necessary to stay true to our first "yes." A Biblical word search will reveal that in the books of Exodus, Leviticus and Numbers, the word "rod" appears 35 times, but that word does not appear even once in the book of Joshua. This indicates a significant shift and transition in the life of the people and even the style and manner of leadership that was necessary. Moses led a movement that centered on an individual. Everything that was done for Israel on their journey prior to Joshua assuming the mantle of leadership as it related to their progress was done by Moses (i.e., plagues, miracles and decision making). Joshua, Moses' successor, had to lead differently. The first words he hears from God upon assuming the leadership mantle of this people moving into the land God promised is, "Moses my servant is dead" (Joshua 1:2). The message is clear: this is a new day! With all due respect to what has transpired in the past, it's now time to chart a new course.

This is exactly what the prophetic element of our ministry is supposed to do. Joshua had to assume the breathtaking task to be both priestly and prophetic in his leadership, keeping the people focused on the traditions handed down to him by Moses (the Commandments were not about to change), and at the same time, moving them forward to the realization and fulfillment of what had been promised but not attained under the leadership of Moses.

What I find most encouraging is that this was a focus and direction in leadership for which the people were clearly ready. There is an interesting, almost startling passage at the end of Joshua 1. In verses 16-18, the people indicate to Joshua that they will follow him wholeheartedly as he follows the commands

God gives. "Just as we fully obeyed Moses, so we will obey you" (although we may leave open to question when we read the Pentateuch how much the people actually obeyed Moses; perhaps Joshua should have asked for a higher standard of loyalty). They imply their weariness with the wanderings in the wilderness that had been their experience for the previous forty years: "Whoever rebels against your word and does not obey your words, whatever you may command them, will be put to death." These are strong words that reflect the great desire of the people to move forward into what they believe God has for them. Apparently, the people understand (finally!) that there are consequences to disobedience, and they want no more of it. They are ready to move into the land God promised, and delays due to disobedience will no longer be tolerated.

I believe that the same situation exists in our church today. There are people who make up the rank and file, those that occupy the pews in our churches, who are in more than a few cases far ahead of the preachers and administrators who lead them. Take for example the instances that are increasingly frequent in the A.M.E. Zion Church, that in many places where an A.M.E. Zion pastor leaves the denomination and starts a church (usually "non-denominational") in the same city, a shocking number of parishioners, once loyal to the A.M.E. Zion Church, follow. The party line that is espoused by those who criticize the departure of the pastor (who may have been once heralded for loyalty and gifts used in the interest of the denomination they have left) is that these people are gullible followers of an "Elmer Gantry" type. The fact that may be conveniently ignored is that some people who leave are being offered something more than what they have seen or received in their previous church experience and they are hungry for something deeper and more fulfilling. For whatever reason they reach this conclusion, these persons do not feel that they are receiving it from the church in its present state. Even if we agree with Bill Hull, who writes, "Believe it or not, people don't usually do a lot of research, and then act in accordance with biblical truth, when choosing to leave a church,"[50]

[50] Bill Hull, *It's Just Not Working,* from "Leadership," Summer, 2005, Vol. XXVI, Number 3, p. 27

we must acknowledge that there must be something deeper taking place when there is a mild (or mass?) exodus from our churches. We cannot continue to make the departures the fault of those who leave. Some of the responsibility lies with us who remain. Like the people of Israel in the book of Joshua, our members are tired of this "wandering around" in the wilderness, and want authentic, godly, visionary leadership. When they grow sufficiently tired of leadership that is misdirected, misguided and injudicious, they leave for something else or something better – in many cases, a leadership that in their estimation is both priestly and prophetic.

This is a day that calls for prophets to stand again and speak boldly for God, men and women who will do the most daring thing imaginable in a church culture that is consumed with the pursuit of an agenda that was not given to us by our Lord. We must get back to where we started, breaking through what Bill Hull calls "the false vision of leadership," where we are guided by

> Church infrastructure, traditions, and institutional community...a leadership model that insists pastors be managers of church growth rather than shepherds helping people go deeper into the life Christ has for us.[51]

We can do it, but the problem we face, as the Lectionary Commentary points out, is how do you find your glasses when you can't find your glasses?

> You need your glasses to find your glasses. If you wear spectacles, you know what I mean. You wake up in the morning, instinctively reach for your

[51] Ibid., p. 26

> glasses on the bed stand next to you, and they're not there. You put them down somewhere different before getting into bed last night, somewhere 'safe,' and now you don't remember the safe place. So you start groping around, feeling the tops of tables and dressers, knocking things over. If you only had your glasses, it would make it a lot easier to find them.[52]

This aptly describes what it is like to find your way back to your first "yes." For many of us, the influences that have held sway over us have left us successful but unfulfilled, and our work and ministry have caused us to function more like strategists than shepherds. I believe that "life as a leader should be a reflection of my relationship to Christ. Leadership is not about

[52] Andre Resner, Jr., "Fourth Sunday After the Epiphany, Year A, in Van Harn, Roger E., editor, *The Lectionary Commentary:* Theological Exegesis for Sunday's Texts (Grand Rapids, Eerdmans Publishing Co., 2001), p. 162

competency and productivity as we have been led to believe."[53]

Reaching this conclusion, the only answer is to find our glasses - struggle through the fumbling and bumbling that marks the process of discovering again what we need in order to see and know our purpose, and get back on track. We are going to have to accept the challenge of being the prophetic voice God has called us to be.

The challenge of the prophet lays in having the courage to know and act on what needs to be passed on, and what needs to be given a decent burial. It is unutterably hard to do this well, because the prophet, as Abraham Heschel points out, speaks "one octave too high" for his

[53] Bill Hull, *It's Just Not Working,* from Leadership, Summer, 2005, Vol. XXVI, Number 3, p. 27

(her) listeners and has no language in common with the audience to whom they speak.[54] You can never adequately explain what you heard from God; you need only be faithful to the word you heard, and know that in proclaiming that word faithfully, God will reward you by performing publicly what God told you privately. God's word is spoken to be spoken. People gather in churches every Sunday, not to hear us, who are mere vessels and conduits of God's message. We are, after all, mortals. People gather at the church in order to hear God. We must speak that word we have received from God with clarity, power and precision, and prove that God will do what God says, because the prophet is, as

[54] Abraham J. Heschel, *The Prophets,* Harper & Row, New York, 1962. P. 9

Harold Kushner says, "not a man who tells the future, he is a man who tells the truth."[55]

To do this, I must find the courage, as Parker J. Palmer says, "to live divided no more." People who achieve this life and sense of calling "have transformed the notion of punishment itself. They have come to understand that *no punishment anyone might inflict on them could possibly be worse than the punishment they inflict on themselves by conspiring in their own diminishment.*"[56]

This explains my journey and present state of mind and affairs. I love the church, my church, the African Methodist Episcopal Zion Church,

[55] Harold S. Kushner, *Living a Life that Matters: Resolving the Conflict Between Conscience and Success,* Alfred A. Knopf, New York, 2001. P. 93
[56] Parker J. Palmer, *Let Your Life Speak: Listening for the Voice of Vocation*. P. 34

the church of my birth and the church to which I have given my life. In my journey, I have made a wonderful and refreshing discovery: I am not here serving the A.M.E. Zion Church because I have no other choice. I love my ministry, the enjoyment it has brought to me, the many ways that I have benefited both personally and professionally, and if I had to start over knowing what I know now, as the song says, "I wouldn't take nothing for my journey." I would do it all over again, so rewarding has this journey been for me.

But I am also tired. I am tired of trying to be what others expect of me when that which they expect is in conflict with what God called me to do. I have struggled with definition of my life and ministry for a very long time. I now have to live up to what I have liked saying because it sounds so independent: "I don't care what people think about me." The fact is that for a long time, I have cared what people thought. Why else would I allow myself to be controlled by the opinions of people rather than what I believed God was calling and directing me to do? I have to get back to my first "yes;" no one wants to follow the kind of preacher of whom W. McFerrin Stowe speaks, who leads a church where "instead of a cross, (they) have a weather vane on top of the steeple."[57] I must be true to what I know my call is.

---

[57] W. McFerrin Stowe, *If I Were a Pastor,* Abingdon Press, Nashville. P.. 38

Chapter 7

I'll Say "Yes"

Now how does it happen that there is no resolving of this contradiction? The No from the earliest days has had on its side much greater power to convince than the Yes has had; what is the reason it cannot once for all submerge the Yes? Why is it that we never break through to the clear and final conclusion that our sense of being inside is mistaken? The answer is hinted at in the very inevitableness of our continued asking for a knowledge of God: we belong to the Yes and not to the No.[58]

I now know that I have some decisions to make. To make these decisions will take

[58] Karl Barth, *The Word of God and the Word of Man,* Peter Smith, Gloucester, Massachusetts, 1978, p. 54

courage on my part, more courage, perhaps, than I have displayed or have been called upon to muster previously to this point on the journey. I will need the courage, if need be, to stand alone, knowing that I am doing what God has called me to do. I will need the courage to understand that when I make a decision in the desire to do God's will, God will indeed take care of me, as I have so often preached and reassured others that God will do. I will need the courage to avoid "believing my own press clippings," as my mother was fond of saying.

In ministry, I am supposed to focus on the imperative and not merely the important. Administrative management is not supposed to be the heartbeat of my ministry; apostolic movement, guided by the Holy Spirit, is.

Success, because it is too ephemeral a goal for which to strive, will not be the driving impetus behind what I do for God; rather, acting in a way so as to be significant is what I want. And I am a priest and prophet in the church. That is what I told the church I wanted to be when I was commissioned by the Quarterly Conference at Mother A.M.E. Zion Church in 1975, when I was ordained to the ministry in 1978, and what I promised I would do when I received each appointment as a pastor of a church since 1982.

It is easy, although not excusable, to understand how we lost our way.

> Pastoral work, in large part, deals with the difficulty everyone has in staying alert to the magnificence of salvation. When we first encounter God's saving love, it may well overwhelm us. But over a period of years it becomes a familiar part of the landscape, one religious item

> among many others. The vocabulary of salvation becomes hackneyed, reduced to the level of valentine-card verse... Whenever we are associated with greatness over a long period of time, there is a tendency in us to become stale. What we first experienced...as earthshaking and soul-changing vision and adventure, we now take for granted. We lose, in the language of the Apocalypse, our 'first love.' We preserve its importance by assigning the event a date on the calendar or by describing it under a doctrinal head. Orthodoxy is preserved even while intimacy is lost.[59]

I do not know if one factor or a series of factors has brought me to this point of awareness, but I am grateful for the revelation. It would be tragic to have a lifetime of ministry end up as a fruitless endeavor because I had stopped paying attention to the signs along the way

[59] Eugene H. Peterson, *Five Smooth Stones for Pastoral Work,* Eerdmans Publishing, Grand Rapids, 1992. P. 31

that indicated that I may have been going in the wrong direction. Carl S. Dudley and Nancy T. Ammerman make an observation about churches that could apply to preachers as well. There are

> Some very clear differences between congregations that embrace change and those that resist or ignore it...One of the first things we discovered about adapting congregations was that they simply notice what is going on around them. Declining congregations barely realize that the world has changed.[60]

The world has changed, I've changed, the people I serve have changed, and if I'm going to be effective in ministry, then I need to pay atten-

[60] Carl S. Dudley and Nancy T. Ammerman, *Congregations in Transition: A Guide for Analyzing, Assessing and Adapting in Changing Communities*, Jossey-Bass, San Francisco, 2002. P. 8

tion. My friend and colleague, Reverend Lester McCorn has observed, correctly, I believe, that

> In addition to the programmatic and liturgical functions of the Church, there has to be a fundamental reform of the poimenic, or pastoral care, practices of the A.M.E. Zion Church...In liberation theology, praxis teaches that liberation only takes place when the practitioner self-consciously becomes an agent of change, and acts to transform and to be transformed by the reality acted upon.[61]

It is so necessary that I go back to what I promised God I would do when I said "yes" for the first time. This is particularly necessary now that things are pulling me in so many different directions. True, it's called life; but it isn't sup-

[61] Lester McCorn, from *A.M.E. Zion Quarterly Review,* January, 2004, Volume CXVI, Number 1, J. David Armstrong, Editor

posed to crowd out the meaning of ministry for me. I need to recover the center.

Perhaps the center just got lost in the busy activity of doing what I was doing. It started out well. With a commission from God that arrived with what I believed was a clear sense of clarity, I answered that call I heard in 1975. I could relate to the seventy that the Lord appointed in Luke 10. Jesus sent them out with directives to go out "like lambs among wolves. Do not take a purse or bag or sandals; and do not greet anyone on the road. When you enter a house, first say, 'Peace to this house.' If a man of peace is there, your peace will rest on him; if not, it will return to you. Stay in that house, eating and drinking whatever they give you, for the worker deserves his wages. Do not move around from house to house. When you enter a town and are welcomed, eat what is set before you. Heal the sick who are there and tell them, 'The kingdom of God is near you'" (Luke 10:3-9).

I laugh at this now, but as I think back on the early days of my ministry, when figuratively or factually speaking I didn't have a clue about what I was doing, I am amazed that there was anything even remotely approaching what might be termed success. On reflection, it seems that what might be termed success was not the goal at all. I was so happy to be included in the endeavor that I was thoroughly consumed with the thought of being a part of the process. I have often likened myself to a middle school student turned loose in a science lab and allowed to perform experiments, filled with glee at all the toys and potions and vials and flasks and gadgets that are now suddenly at my disposal! Now, I look back with gratitude that the concoctions I put together and the solutions I tried didn't blow up the lab! I know the joy that the seventy must have felt when they came back to Jesus after a time in the field doing ministry and brought the report, "Lord, even the demons submit to us in your name!" (Luke 10:17).

So far, so good; now the question is how do we sustain this momentum? How do we keep the thrust and the forward push?

The answer to this question comes for us at the end of Luke 10, when the scene shifts to the home of a woman named Martha. She and her sister Mary and brother Lazarus were all friends of Jesus, dear friends, in fact. The mind races to think about what the conversation must have been like when Jesus went to this home, a place where he could relax and unwind. He comes here to get away from the demands of people, to hide from the arguments that the religious leaders constantly seek to trap him in some misquote or mistake in interpretation of the law. I picture this as a place where Jesus can put his feet up on the sofa and chill out.

Martha is a perfectionist. She wants everything to be exactly right, just so. Even though Jesus is a frequent guest, just like family, it doesn't mean she wants to slack at all in the preparations. She will not have him come to her house and have to say, "Oh, Jesus, excuse the mess." Oh, no, she will have everything in place and in order. So she's running around, hustling all over the house, fixing things, moving things, barking orders, slamming pots and throwing things around to create just the right ambiance for Jesus.

In the meantime, Jesus arrives and finds his favorite and most comfortable chair. It doesn't bother Martha at first because Jesus is a frequent guest. Dinner is almost ready anyway, so he won't have to wait long. But then something does bother her. She looks in the sitting room and sees her sister, Mary. And she is not happy at all about what she sees. Mary is sitting on the floor in front of Jesus with her mouth wide open, hanging on every word he speaks. Ordinarily, Martha wouldn't mind. I sort of imagine Martha thinking or saying that Mary kind of gets in the way anyway, and she never quite folds the napkins correctly or has the tablecloth measured exactly the right distance from the chairs so it's not getting in the way of the table guests - but there are things to be done! There is no time for her to just sit around talking.

The gentle clearing of her throat is not working, and the constant moving past the room and giving Mary that look isn't doing much good either. So finally Martha decides it's time to say something. She is trying to be as polite as possible, but clearly she is annoyed, and as you can imagine, it shows in the tone of her voice when she speaks. She probably says the words slowly, very slowly, and carefully for emphasis: "Lord, don't you care that my sister has left me to do all the work by myself? Tell her to help me!"

She expects Mary to jump up immediately and get in the kitchen and start some task but she doesn't move. Jesus' intentions are not to meddle in the middle of a sibling argument, but rather to put this situation in perspective. So he says to Martha, "Martha, Martha, you are worried and upset about many things, but only one thing is needed. Mary has chosen what is better, and it will not be taken away from her" (Luke 10:41-42).

Well, this simplifies things considerably. "Only one thing is needed..." I can see how there must be a process of elimination for me to be faithful to the spirit of my first "yes." This one needed thing is God's word. The hustling and bustling is not needed. Activity is not the same thing as ministry and activity without ministry, that is, something done with a sense of purpose, is frustrating. Mary chose the good part because she was able to hear things that she was not able to hear while Martha was running around the kitchen. And what Mary heard at the feet of Jesus we learn "could not be taken away from her." In addition, there is a striking element of this story, that women were not taught, and especially not by any rabbi of esteem. Mary exhibits real courage because she was willing to risk the unconventional to get from Jesus what she wanted. This is the kind of courage that those who want to follow their first "yes" must display.

I'm thinking now of October of 1982, by which time it had become clear to me what I should do, and I guess that I acquiesced to the track on which the A.M.E. Zion Church placed most of its preachers. I have no regrets about this now. I am not unhappy about nor do I have any remorse about the decision to be a pastor. In fact, it is a decision that has brought me immeasurable joy and satisfaction. I was appointed by Bishop Speaks to Pierce Chapel A.M.E. Zion Church in Clarkton, North Carolina. And thus began my life as a pastor.

I arrived there that first Sunday of my new pastorate filled with more hope and fear than I have ever known in my life on any given day. Although I was nervous, I covered it up admirably, I hope. I tried to give the impression of confidence, poise and self-assurance. One of my dearest and best friends, Rev. W. Darin Moore went with me. I remember that Darin offered the Morning Prayer in the worship. After his prayer I felt better; a huge burden seemed to lift from me. After the prayer, the doors to the sanctuary opened and my mother, father and two grandmothers entered the church. I knew then that everything was going to be all right.

The congregation received me well that day. I later learned, somewhat to my surprise, that they did not want me to come as their pastor. Their plan was, I was told, to give me a week's salary and send me on my way with sincere thanks. They did not like that the bishop had issued an edict at the previous Annual Conference that they would be a "station" church, as opposed to a "circuit" church (they previously had worship on second and fourth Sundays only, which defines a "circuit" church). Something changed their mind, and I was glad for that. It was the beginning of a relatively fruitful three year ministry stint at that church.

So I journey on. I hear the voice again clearly that commissioned me in 1975. It is as distinct and as apparent and comprehensible as I believed it to be then. The only difference is that now I have some thirty years of experience behind me as I seek to be what I believe God has called me to be. I recognize that I cannot be what others expect or want, mainly because their expectations are too low. God has something glorious and lofty in mind for me, and I do not wish to settle for anything less. It is exciting to realize that

> God has been at work with this person (me) since birth. Everything that has taken place in this life has in some